OXFORD
INDIA SHORT
INTRODUCTIONS

# THE RIGHT TO INFORMATION IN INDIA

The Oxford India Short
Introductions are concise,
stimulating, and accessible guides
to different aspects of India.
Combining authoritative analysis,
new ideas, and diverse perspectives,
they discuss subjects which are
topical yet enduring, as also
emerging areas of study and debate.

OXFORD
INDIA SHORT
INTRODUCTIONS

# THE RIGHT TO
# INFORMATION
# IN INDIA

SUDHIR NAIB

OXFORD
UNIVERSITY PRESS

OXFORD
UNIVERSITY PRESS

Oxford University Press is a department of the University of Oxford.
It furthers the University's objective of excellence in research, scholarship,
and education by publishing worldwide. Oxford is a registered trademark of
Oxford University Press in the UK and in certain other countries

Published in India by
Oxford University Press
2/11 Ground Floor, Ansari Road, Daryaganj, New Delhi 110 002, India

© Oxford University Press 2013

The moral rights of the author have been asserted

First Edition published in 2013

ISBN-13: 978-0-19-808935-3
ISBN-10: 0-19-808935-X

Typeset in 11/15.6 Bembo Std
by Excellent Laser Typesetters, Pitampura, Delhi 110 034
Printed in India by Replika Press Pvt. Ltd

*To*
*My courageous mother Asha Rani Naib,*
*my loving sister Vishu Bhalla to whom more*
*is owed than can be said in words, and*
*memory of my father Wazir Chand Naib*

# Contents

# Figures and Tables

## Figures

## Tables

# Introduction

The Supreme Court of India had recognized the right to information as a constitutionally-protected fundamental right. In *State of Uttar Pradesh v. Raj Narain and Others*, Justice K.K. Mathew observed:

> In a government of responsibility like ours, where all the agents of the public must be responsible for their conduct, there can be but a few secrets. The people of this country have a right to know every public act, everything that is done in a public way by their public functionaries. They are entitled to know the particulars of every public transaction in all its bearings.

Further, in *S.P. Gupta v. Union of India*, Justice P.N. Bhagwati observed:

> The concept of an open Government is the direct emanation from the right to know which seems to

be implicit in the right of free speech and expression guaranteed under Article 19(1)(a). Therefore, disclosure of information in regard to the functioning of the Government must be the rule and secrecy an exception justified only where the strictest requirement of public interest so demands. The approach of the Court must be to attenuate the area of secrecy as much as possible consistently with the requirement of public interest, bearing in mind all the time that disclosure also serves an important aspect of public interest. (p. 234)

Despite all this, however, there was little effort by the government to institutionalize, and set up a legal framework to exercise the right to information. It was in the 1990s when various people's movements, most prominent among them being the Mazdoor Kisan Shakti Sangathan (MKSS), put concerted and sustained pressure to build up such an institution. It is a marvel that such a law could be passed despite resistance from a large number of vested interests. This happened due to a number of factors, such as mass mobilization of rural populations, building of alliances amongst different movements to join hands and recognize the right to information as a priority for all, and intense lobbying by activists with political leaders. And then came a change in the Government. The United Progressive Alliance (UPA) came to power in May 2004 and its Common Minimum Programme (CMP) stated to make the Right to Information Act 'more progressive, participatory and meaningful'. The UPA government set up the National Advisory Council (NAC) to monitor the implementation of the CMP. The Council was chaired by Sonia Gandhi and had leaders of various people's movements, including the right to information movement, as members. Finally, the Right to Information Bill was passed by the Parliament in May 2005, and got the President's assent on 15 June 2005.

The Right to Information (RTI) law granting citizens legal right to access information made the governments increase transparency in its functioning. The law is internationally recognized as being among the most powerful transparency laws in the world.

For about seven years, the RTI law has been used extensively by ordinary citizens to demand different kinds of information, albeit with the help of civil society groups in many instances. RTI is being used to redress individual grievances, access entitlements such as ration cards, and so on, to investigate government policies and decisions, and expose corruption/misuse of public money. To many, particularly the poor and disadvantaged, the act of filing an RTI application itself is empowering and often leads to the resolution of their problems. Civil society organizations have played an important role in raising public awareness about the RTI. In recent times, although there appears to be a decline in petty corruption, increased big ticket corruption as evident from major scandals like the 2G, the Commonwealth Games, and the Adarsh Housing Society, were unearthed by use of the RTI. A number of activists who have made significant contributions in this movement include Anna Hazare, Arvind Kejriwal, Aruna Roy, Nikhil Dey, Subhash Agarwal, Anjali Bhardwaj, Shekhar Singh, Maja Daruwala, and Venkatesh Nayak of the Commonwealth Human Rights Initiative, to name a few.

To a vast majority of Indians, the RTI is a new sense of empowerment that, for the first time, allows them a legal right to 'demand' information and to receive it in time-bound manner. It gives them the right to have an official penalized for providing wrong information, or delaying the process in an undue manner, or denying information itself in the first place. Ultimately, this

sense of empowerment also spills over to ~~c~~
tions that the common man enters into with
They look at the government functionary as someone
who is answerable to them, and not someone they
are answerable to, as was the case in past. That is the
game changer!

The RTI has now become a national movement in
India, and has set an example for such other rights–based
legislations. These include the Right to Employment,
the Right to Education, the Right to Food, the Right
of Citizens for Time Bound Delivery of Goods and
Services and Redressal of their Grievances, and the
Electronic Delivery of Services. Also, Whistleblowers
Protection Bill, Judicial Accountability Bill, and the
Lokpal may help reinforce transparency and account-
ability in governance.

This short introduction comprises seven chapters.
The first chapter, 'Freedom of Information: A Global
Perspective', provides an overview of the law in vari-
ous countries in Europe, the Americas (USA, Canada,
Mexico), Asia-Pacific (Pakistan, Bangladesh), and
Africa. A comparative analysis of different Freedom
of Information (FOI) laws based on their common
features like the Right to Access Information, Scope

of Coverage, Methods of Processing Information, Proactive Disclosure, Exemptions from Disclosure, Appeal Procedure, and Provision regarding Sanctions, is also attempted in the chapter.

The second, 'Towards Right to Information in India', traces the long journey till its culmination in the law. It starts with the pronouncement of the Supreme Court that the right is a part of the fundamental rights guaranteed under the Indian Constitution, and then explores the people's movements in demanding this right. It also looks into the deliberations of the Parliamentary Standing Committee on the two draft bills—*Freedom of Information Bill* and *Right to Information Bill*.

The third chapter, 'Right to Information Act 2005', starts with an overview of the Act, and then elaborates upon how it has helped people. The chapter also looks at some of the important impact studies on implementation of the Act. Some states, like Andhra Pradesh and Bihar have taken innovative steps in this regard. Further, issues in implementation of the Act are discussed.

The fourth chapter, 'Right of Information Seekers', examines the various rights conferred on citizens under the Act, the kind of information they can seek, and the process for making a request for information and appeal.

The fifth, 'Duties of Information Suppliers', examines the meaning of a 'public authority' and its obligations under the Act. Next, it looks at the duties and responsibilities of public information officers in detail.

The sixth chapter, 'Information Exempted from Disclosure', deals with each of the exemptions and elaborates upon them with case laws on the subject.

The seventh chapter, 'Recommendations to Improve Implementation of Right to Information', discusses relevant issues on the subject and makes recommendations for effective implementation.

There are a number of booklets and handbooks on the Right to Information available in the public domain. The various guides for all stakeholders can be accessed at http://rti.gov.in. The government guidelines and orders with respect to right to information can be accessed from the nodal department, Department of Personnel and Training (DoPT) at http://persmin.nic.in. The decisions of the Central Information Commission (CIC) are available on http://www.cic.gov.in/. The other useful resources on the web are Centre for Good Governance at http://www.cgg.gov.in and Commonwealth Human Rights Initiative at http://www.humanrightsinitiative.org/.

# 1

# Freedom of Information

## A Global Perspective

Freedom of Information (FOI) as a tool to make a government accountable is not a recent phenomenon. Sweden has the oldest legislation relating to public access to official documents. The Swedish Freedom of the Press Act, adopted in 1766, set the principle that government records were by default to be made accessible to the public and granted citizens the right to demand documents from government bodies, which were prepared and received by them. For this, Swedish citizens did not have to provide a reason. Documents that were to be exempted from disclosure were defined in the Secrecy Act and even under this Act; they were secret only for a specified period of time.

However, for over a century, Sweden remained the only nation that took to transforming this principle into a legal right. It was not until the creation of the United Nations (in the period following the Second World War) that the concept of the right to information began to spread, and countries began to enact comprehensive laws for public access to government-held documents and information. Article 19 of the Universal Declaration of Human Rights in 1948 called for all persons to have a right to seek and receive information. Soon after, many Nordic countries began to look at the Swedish model. Finland, for instance, enacted the Law on the Public Character of Official Documents in 1951. Norway and Denmark passed their Information access laws in 1970. In the next 30 years, they were followed by the United States Freedom of Information Act in 1966, France and the Netherlands in 1978, Australia and New Zealand in 1982, and Canada in 1983. The UK's Freedom of Information Act 2000 was fully implemented in January 2005.

Over time, FOI laws have become increasingly common across the globe. Over 80 countries around the world have now adopted comprehensive FOI Acts to facilitate access to records held by government bodies and many others are making efforts towards it. Some of them, such as Bolivia, Guatemala, Pakistan, and Philippines have issued decrees or used constitutional provisions to provide access to such records. However, the culture of secrecy remains strong in many countries and several such laws, therefore, remain inadequate. In spite of these problems, more information is being released into the public domain as FOI legislation helps create a greater culture of openness.

# Regional Trends in Adoption of FOI Laws

## *Europe*

In Europe, nearly all nations have adopted FOI laws. Many Western European countries adopted these laws starting from the 1970s. In Central and Eastern Europe, for instance, the change was more dramatic. The breakdown of the USSR led to a rush of laws in the region starting with Ukraine and Hungary in 1992, Azerbaijan in 2005, and Macedonia in 2006. However, Russia and Belarus remain among the larger states which are without FOI laws. The organization which played an important role in propagating FOI laws in Europe is George Soros's Open Society Institute (OSI), which took the lead in promoting transparency.

The following section will primarily focus on the United Kingdom's Freedom of Information Act 2000, in some detail.

The United Kingdom adopted the Freedom of Information Act in November 2000, which became fully effective in January 2005. It may be noted that countries like Australia, Canada, and New Zealand had passed the FOI laws in early 1980s. This relatively late adoption of the law by UK came despite strong demands by civil society groups. One of the election promises of the Labour party—which rose to power in 1997, after a long period of Conservative rule—was to adopt a right to information legislation, which was eventually completed in 2000. However, after the 11 September 2001 attack in United States, the UK government delayed implementation of the key elements of the law until January 2005.

The Act provides that any person 'making a request for information to a public authority is entitled' to be informed whether or not the body holds the information and, if it does, to have the information

4

communicated to him [Section 1(1)]. However this right is subject to other provisions in the Act, like the regime of exemptions, payment of any fees, and an exception for vexatious or repeated requests.

The Act defines information as 'information recorded in any form' [Section 84] which is held by the public body at the time of receiving a request [Section 1(4)]. The Act also provides that information is understood to be held by a public authority if, (a) it is held by the authority, or (b) it is held by another person on behalf of the authority [Section 3(2)]. Thus, public authorities cannot escape their obligations by getting someone else to hold the information.

The public authorities are also listed in Schedule 1. The list includes all government departments, the various legislative bodies (other than Scotland, which has its own law), the armed forces, and the numerous other authorities listed individually by name. The Act also provides that the Secretary of State may add to or remove from the list of authorities in Schedule 1, subject to certain conditions [Section 4], or more generally, designate as public authorities those which 'exercise functions of a public nature' or provide contract services for a public body [Section 5]. The Act also provides that where an authority is designated as a public authority only in relation to certain information, the obligation of disclosure is similarly restricted to that particular information [Section 7]. This implies that if an authority is responsible for a certain piece of information, its obligation lies in disclosing only that piece of information.

The Act contains two separate systems for fees. One is for 'ordinary' requests and the other comes into play for more complicated requests. For the first, public authorities may disclose information only after the payment of a fee and any such fee must be paid within three months [Section 9(2)]. Such fees must be in accordance with regulations made by the Secretary of State. These may prescribe that no fee is to be paid in certain cases, set a maximum fee, and/or provide for the manner in which fees are to be calculated. Regulations adopted in 2004 provide that only the costs that may be charged are of informing the applicant that the authority holds the information and communicating the information to him or her (including reproduction and postage or other transmission costs), but not for staff time.

The second fee system as per Section 12 (exemption where cost of compliance exceeds appropriate limit) comes into play when the cost of providing information would exceed such 'appropriate limit ... as may be prescribed'. The 2004 Regulations set this limit at £600 for the central government and the parliament and £450 for the public sector. In calculating the costs, the time spent determining whether the information is held and the time spent locating, retrieving, and extracting the information may be charged at £25 per hour [paragraph 4]. Where the costs would exceed the limit, the public authority is not under any obligation to provide the information although, as per Section 13, it may still provide it and charge all the costs noted earlier, as well as the costs of reproducing and communicating the information to the applicant (paragraph 7 of the Regulations).

Section 19 of the FOI Act provides that every pubic authority must develop, publish, and implement a publication scheme setting out the classes of information which it will publish, the manner in which it will publish them, and whether or not it intends to charge for any particular publication. The scheme must be approved by the Information Commissioner. The Code of Practice published by the Secretary of State sets out some specific, proactive publication duties, including the publishing of procedures for dealing with requests for information.

Under Section 1 of the Act, public authorities have two distinct duties—the duty to confirm or deny [Section 1(1)(a)] and the duty to communicate information [Section 1(1)(b)]. As a general rule, each specific exempting provision within Part II of the Act specifies separately the circumstances in which each duty is excluded.

Broadly, the exemptions can fall in two categories: absolute and qualified. Where information falls within the scope of an 'absolute exemption', a public authority is not obliged to communicate it to an applicant. Also, in most absolute exemptions, the authority will be excused from the obligation to confirm or deny. However, when the requested information falls within the scope of 'qualified exemption', a public authority must comply with its duties under Section 1(1) unless public interest in non-disclosure outweighs the public interest in disclosure [Section 2].

The absolute exemptions are listed under Section 2(3). In these exemptions, public authority need not consider whether public interest favours disclosure. The Information Commissioner has no power to disclose in 'public interest', if the information falls within the scope of absolute exemption.

In the case of qualified exemptions, the public authority must consider the competing public interests in disclosure and the maintenance of secrecy.

In all, there are three general exemptions and 20 specific exemptions. The three general exemptions are for vexatious or repeated requests [Section 14], information which is already reasonably accessible to the applicant even though this involves payment [Section 21—absolute exemption], and information intended to be published as long as it is reasonable not to disclose it as per the request, even though no date of publication has been set [Section 22].

The FOI Act has three levels of appeal. First, within the public authority which holds the information, second to the Information Commission (IC), and then to the Information Tribunal. When the IC orders the release of information based on the public interest test, the decision can be overruled with a ministerial certificate. The certificate is to be announced in Parliament and under the law is subject to judicial review. The Tribunal has the power to review decisions of the IC on both points of law and fact [Sections 57–8]. A further appeal may be made by the courts regarding the decision of the Tribunal, on points of law [Section 59] (for details see Wadham and Griffiths 2005).

## *Americas*

In this regard, the United States of America's legislation is an innovative act and has given the rest of the world 40 years of experience to draw on. There is a long history of access to public records in the United States—some states have provided access to records for over a century. The US Freedom of Information Act was enacted in 1966 and went into effect the year after. In addition, all 50 individual states currently have a right to information law of their own. The FOI Act has been substantially amended several times. The law allows any person or organization, regardless of citizenship, to ask for records held by Federal government agencies. These agencies include executive and military departments, government corporations and other entities which perform government functions except for the Congress, the Courts, or the President's immediate staff at the White House, as well as the National Security Council. The law is, therefore, focused on the executive branch of the government and does not cover either the legislative branch—the Congress—or the Courts. Moreover, the government agencies must respond within 20 working days (Baniser 2006: 158–61).

There are nine categories of discretionary exemptions: national security, internal agency rules, information protected by other statutes, business information, inter- and intra-agency memos, personal privacy, law enforcement records, financial institutions, and oil well data. However, since 11 September 2001, the US Government passed certain legislations such as USA PATRIOT (Uniting and Strengthening America by Providing Appropriate Tools Required to Intercept and Obstruct Terrorism) Act 2001, the Homeland Security Act 2002, and other non-legislative measures which limited the access to sensitive and potentially sensitive information. There has also been an unprecedented process of reclassification wherein thousands of declassified documents at National Archives and Records Administrative (NARA) have since been reclassified. As per M. Aid's (2006) *Declassification in Reverse*, this process has resulted in the reclassification of 9,500 documents (55,000 pages). Thus, there have been significant changes in the balance between people's right to know and national security since 11 September 2001.

The United States FOI Act has both strengths and weaknesses. The strengths include good provisions on fees, strong rules on the electronic provision of information, and a number of good promotional measures such as mandatory declassification review, whereby an individual may request declassification review of specific classified material. The weaknesses include the Act's applicability to only federal agencies and not to records held by Congress, the courts, or by state or local government agencies. However, it is fair to say that a reasonable degree of openness has developed in the government, not only by the FOI Act, but also by the activities of whistleblowers as well as the Privacy Act, which provides access to personal information held by public authorities.

The Canadian Access to Information Act 1983 provides Canadian citizens and corporations in Canada the right to apply for and obtain copies of records held by government institutions. These institutions must reply in 15 days. Records can be withheld for a number of reasons if they: were obtained in confidence from a foreign government, international organization, provincial, municipal, or regional government; injure federal–provincial or international affairs or national defence; relate to legal investigations, trade secrets, financial, commercial, scientific, or technical information belonging to the government or materially injurious to the financial interests of Canada; include personal information defined by the Privacy Act; contain trade secrets and other confidential information of third parties; or relate to operations of the government that are less than 20 years old. Documents designated as cabinet confidences are excluded from the Act and are presumed secret for 20 years (Baniser 2006: 54–7). Appeals of withholding are made to the Office of the Information Commissioner of Canada. The Commissioner receives complaints and can investigate and issue recommendations, but does not have the power to issue a binding order. The Act was amended by the Terrorism Act in November 2001. The amendments allow the Attorney General to issue a certificate to bar an investigation by the Information Commission regarding information obtained in confidence from a 'foreign entity'. This is done keeping in mind the protection of national security, in case the Commissioner has ordered the release of information.

Moreover, a provision for limited judicial review is also provided for.

Mexico's Federal Transparency and Access to Public Government Information law was passed in April 2002 which came into effect in June 2003. It has taken the lead with one of the strongest laws in the world, overseen by an Information Commission and an advanced information system which keeps track of all requests and ensures that they are answered on time. Similar laws have also been adopted in Jamaica, Trinidad and Tobago, Belize, Panama, Peru, Ecuador, the Dominican Republic, and Antigua and Barbuda. Executive decrees giving a limited right of access have been issued in Argentina, Bolivia, and Guatemala. In many of these countries, pressure has come from the World Bank and other lenders as part of anti-corruption measures. The Organization of American States also released a draft bill in 2000.

### Asia–Pacific

In the Asia–Pacific region, Australia and New Zealand were the original adopters and South Korea and Thailand followed in the 1990s. Japan adopted a national law in 2000 and nearly 3,000 localities have their own laws. In India, following the adoption of such laws in a number of states, a national law was adopted in 2002 but was not implemented. It was replaced in 2005 by a stronger law.

The Indian Right to Information (RTI) Act 2005 is limited to citizens. It extends to the whole of India, apart from the state of Jammu and Kashmir, which has its own information law. The RTI Act 2005 is binding on both national and state governments. The Act provides for the appointment of both Central and State Public Information Officers (PIOs), as well as the establishment of both Central and State Information Commissioners. The main exemptions are given in Section 8 of the Act, which are largely consistent with other right to information laws. Section 24 provides for the exclusion of a number of intelligence and security bodies from the ambit of the Act. Under Section 22, the provisions of the Act shall have effect in spite of any inconsistency they may have with the Official Secrets Act 1923 or any other law for the time being in force. On the whole, the Indian law is a comprehensive one.

In other countries in this region, Pakistan has a Freedom of Information Ordinance, 2002 while, in

October 2011, a Right to Information Bill was also moved as a private member bill by Ms Sherry Rehman in the National Assembly. Sri Lanka too, has a private member bill moved in 2011. In the Maldives, the RTI bill has been pending in Parliament since 2009 and Bangladesh has passed the RTI Act in 2009. Civil society advocates in Indonesia, Malaysia, and Cambodia are now pushing for the adoption of similar laws. In the former Soviet Republics in Central Asia, access remains largely illusory, although such laws have been adopted in Uzbekistan and Tajikistan.

## Middle East

In the Middle East, only Israel has adopted such a national law. There are also efforts pending in Jordan and Palestine and similar developments in Morocco and Egypt.

## Africa

In Africa, the progress has been slow. Many development agencies have been pressuring countries to adopt laws as a part of anti-corruption measures. In South Africa, for instance, the 'Promotion of Access to Information Act' was passed in February 2000 and implemented in March 2001. It has some progressive features which allows for access to records held by private bodies if it affects an individual's rights. Also, it imparts legal protection to those people, who, for example, provide information about corruption cases. The South African law has very strong procedural guarantees, as well as a narrowly-crafted set of exemptions. However, a major shortcoming of the law is that it does not provide for an administrative level of appeal. Therefore, if a request for information is refused, only the courts can review it.

Angola adopted a law in 2002 largely based on the Portuguese law, but is yet to implement it. Uganda adopted the FOI in May 2005. In Zimbabwe, the cynically-named Access to Information and Protection of Privacy Act is used only to suppress the media (Baniser 2006: 20).

## A Comparative Study of FOI Laws

Most countries across the globe have recognized the individuals' right to information held by public bodies.

A comparative study of FOI laws of various countries indicates reasonable consistency (Mendel 2008: 141–54). Also, it is seen that a few countries have adopted more innovative approaches. The following section presents a comparative analysis of the FOI laws.

## *Right to Access Information*

The right to access information held by public bodies is the fundamental reason for passing a right to information law. Many legislations begin with the purpose for such a law. This is useful in clarifying the underpinnings of the law and as an interpretive tool. The general principles that are found in different laws include promoting a transparent, accountable, and an effective government, controlling corruption, fostering public participation, and building public understanding and an informed citizenery.

Some laws also include a number of more pragmatic provisions among their principles, such as practical mechanisms for accessing information, and ensuring that access is rapid and inexpensive.

South Africa provides for a right of access to documents or records while most others provide for a right of access to information. This distinction is significant. When the law provides a right of access to 'information' and not to 'documents' or 'records', the applicant is not required to specify any particular document or record. However, most countries today interpret the words 'information' and 'record' quite liberally in their FOI laws. Currently, most laws broadly define the right to include all information, irrespective of the medium it is stored in. For example, in India, the RTI Act allows individuals to demand samples such as food that is distributed or materials used to make roads.

In most cases, the right applies to all information regardless of the purpose for which it is held. However, some laws—such as those of Jamaica, Mexico, and Japan—restrict the scope, for example, to information held for official purposes or in connection with the functions of the public body. Such restrictions limit the right to information. They have no legitimate basis since the right to information should not depend on the deemed usefulness or role of the information. It has value in itself.

All laws apply to information 'held' by a public authority. Some laws—such as those of Peru and the United States—also require that the information be under the 'control'of the public body. To understand the difference, let us take an example where copies of information have been passed on to a number of different public authorities. Each will then 'hold' the information and there will be no need to engage in establishing which authority is in 'control' of the information.

Other laws extend to information that may be accessed by a public body. The Indian law, for example, applies to information relating to any private body which can be accessed by a public authority under any other law for the time being in force. The law of the United Kingdom also applies to information held by another person on behalf of a public authority.

## *Scope of Coverage*

To define which authorities are covered by a right to information law, there are two main approaches. First, is to simply define the authorities covered and then let any controversial issue be decided as per the facts of the case. This is the most common approach. Second, some laws provide a list of authorities which fall within their purview. The United Kingdom law uses this approach. However, in such instances, each time an authority is created or changes its name or modifies its purpose or structure, the schedule needs to be updated either by the Parliament or through regulation. Perhaps a better solution would be to combine both approaches, that is, providing a generic definition of authorities, but also listing authorities which are specifically covered.

In many countries like India, all three branches of government—administrative, legislative, and judicial—fall within the scope of these laws, while in others, such as the United States and Japan, it is restricted to the executive. In some cases such as South Africa, Thailand, and Jamaica, the law covers the courts but only with respect to their administrative functions.

The scope of many laws extends beyond public corporations and includes private bodies which receive funding through public contracts or which otherwise carry out public functions. The Indian law, for example, applies to bodies which are owned, controlled, or substantially financed by the government. It also applies to non-government organizations financed directly or indirectly by funds provided by government. The Bangladesh law extends to private organizations or institutions run by government financing or with aid-in-grant from a government fund, or by foreign aid in grant, and those that undertake public functions in accordance with any contract made on behalf of the Government or made with any public organisation or institution. In South Africa, coverage is extended to all bodies exercising public power or performing a public function as per any legislation.

In most countries, anyone, regardless of citizenship, can claim the right to information, although in some this right is restricted to citizens or residents.

## *Processing Requests for Information*

Mostly, such laws provide for requests to be made in writing, with the name and contact details of the applicant, along with a sufficiently detailed description of the information sought. In some countries, such as South Africa, Azerbaijan, and Kyrgyzstan, applicants can make oral requests by telephone. In most countries, no reason needs to be given for seeking information. Most laws also provide for assistance to be offered to applicants on grounds of either illiteracy or disability. The Indian law provides that the Information Officer shall render all reasonable assistance to the person making the request orally, to reduce the same in writing. Another trend which is emerging is that applicants are now increasingly able to request information using electronic mail or web-based forms. This is not only limited to developed countries—such a system is in place in Turkey, and even Mexico.

Most laws provide for time limits (mostly 30 days) for responding to the request for information. Almost all laws allow for an extension of the time limit, since in instances where the request is a complex one, it requires a search through records not located at the main office or requires consultations with others. Time taken by applicants to respond to questions for clarification or to pay a fee is not taken into account in determining the response time. In several countries, a failure to respond within the time limits constitutes a deemed refusal of the request.

In case of an urgent situation, a shorter time limit is set for providing information. In India, a 48-hour time limit applies wherever the information sought for concerns the life and liberty of a person.

The United Kingdom provides for a longer time limit, where the matter of public interest is concerned.

Longer time limits also apply in a number of countries including India, when a third party notice is required.

Most countries provide for the transfer of requests, or for the applicant to be notified where information is held by another authority. In some cases—such as India, Jamaica, South Africa, and Thailand—the public authority which has received the original request effects the transfer, while in others—such as Mexico— the applicant is simply informed.

Provisions regarding fees vary as per different laws. In most countries this is restricted to the cost of reproducing the information. Many countries also provide for fee waivers for the poor, like that in India and South Africa. In some countries, different fees apply to different sorts of information. For example, the United States law distinguishes between commercial requesters, who may be charged for search, duplication, and review of documents, educational or scientific institutions, which may be charged only for duplication, and other requesters, who may be charged for search and duplication. For the two latter groups, there is waiver for the first two hours of search and 100 pages of copying. Fees are effectively waived for public interest requests, which covers the media and many NGOs.

## *Proactive Disclosure*

It is being increasingly recognized by most countries that proactive disclosure is potent in promoting access to information held by public authorities. As such, many national FOI laws impose a duty on government agencies to release on their own, certain categories of information on their websites. Many of these recent laws, such as those of Peru (2002), Azerbaijan (2005), India (2005), Kyrgyzstan (2007), and Bangladesh (2009) have extensive rules on proactive publication.

It is generally believed that as the number of documents directly accessible to the public increases, the number of requests for information decreases. This *suo motu* disclosure can also improve the efficiency of public bodies.

## *Exemptions from Disclosure*

Almost all FOI laws contain provisions regarding information that may be withheld from release. There are a number of common exemptions found in nearly all laws. These include the protection of national security and international relations, personal privacy, commercial confidentiality, law enforcement and public order, information received in confidence, and internal discussions. In many parliamentary systems, documents that are submitted to the Cabinet for decisions and records of Cabinet meetings are excluded for a specified period of time.

A few laws contain peculiar exemptions. For example, the laws of the United Kingdom and Thailand contain exemptions relating to the royal family. The United States law contains an exemption relating to information about oil wells. The Indian law contains an exemption for information which could lead to incitement of an offence.

A difficult issue is the relationship of right to information with secrecy laws. In most countries, right to information laws do not hinder secrecy laws, although in South Africa and India, the right to information has an overriding force.

The laws of a few countries including the United Kingdom, India, South Africa, Uganda, Azerbaijan, and Japan have general public interest overrides. In India, it applies to all exemptions except where providing access would involve an infringement of copyright of a person other than the state. Most of the laws require that once the harm has lessened, the information should be released. For this, a certain time period is given. In Mexico, the Federal Transparency Act requires that the exemptions apply for 12 years and in India, most of the exemptions are not valid after 20 years. Also, all laws provide for the partial release of information (severability) which does not come under exemption in a document.

A common exemption relates to internal decision-making as the government needs to be able to run its internal operations without undue hindrance. In Bangladesh, file notings are not disclosable whereas in India they are.

A number of laws completely exclude certain bodies from the ambit of the law. Security or intelligence bodies are excluded in the United Kingdom, India, and Peru. However, in India, the exemption does not apply to information relating to corruption and human rights violations.

A number of countries also exclude certain types of requests. In Mexico, for example, offensive requests or requests which have already been dealt with are excluded. In the United Kingdom, vexatious or repeated requests, requests for information which is already accessible, and requests for information intended to be published are excluded. Information about to be published and frivolous or vexatious requests are also excluded in South Africa. This appears to be in order as vexatious, offensive, or repeated requests can impose a costly burden on public authorities and yet not advance the right to information. However, when applied too broadly, they can pose a problem.

## *Appeals*

There are a variety of mechanisms for appeals. These include administrative reviews, court reviews, or oversight by independent bodies. The first level of appeal in nearly all countries is an internal review. This typically involves a higher level entity within the body where the request was made. However, the experience in many countries is that the internal system tends to uphold the denials.

Once the internal appeals have been completed, the next stage is to appeal to an external body. A growing trend is to create an independent Information Commission. These act more informally than a court and may function better for appeals due to their specialized nature. In Australia, there is the Administrative Appeals Tribunal, and in Japan there is the Information Disclosure Review Board, both of which deal with appeals of initial decisions by agencies. In the UK, there is both a Commission and a Review Panel for this purpose. In India, there is the Central Information Commission (CIC), notified by the central government and State Information Commissions in all the states. The final level of review in almost all countries is an appeal to the judiciary.

In most countries, the laws provide that the onus is on the public authority to justify any refusal to provide information.

## Sanctions and Protections

Sanctions are a necessary part of every law to showcase the seriousness of failure to comply. Most FOI laws include provisions for imposing sanctions on public authorities and employees in cases where information is unlawfully withheld. Typically, the cases involve unreasonable refusal to release information, delay in providing information, and altering or destroying documents. These sanctions can be imposed against the body itself or against specific employees responsible for malfeasance.

Most laws provide for fines and even imprisonment for extreme violations. The Polish Law on Access to Public Information states that 'whoever, in spite of his obligation does not provide access to public information, shall be liable to a fine, restricted freedom or imprisonment for up to a year.'

In India, Information Commissioners have imposed fines on Information Officers who have refused or unduly delayed releasing information under the RTI Act. Sanctions that compensate the requestor can also be imposed against bodies that refuse to release information.

Many laws also provide for protection for good faith disclosures under the law. A number of countries including India, South Africa, and Uganda protect officials against any form of liability for acts done in the performance of a duty under the law. Some countries hold officials liable for disclosing exempt information. The Swedish law, for example, provides for liability under the penal code and also imposes some form of direct liability. Under the Mexican law, officials are administratively liable for wrongful disclosures, while in Jamaica, officials remain legally liable for disclosures which breach the right to information.

Laws in some countries, like that of Uganda, United Kingdom, South Africa, and the United States provide for the protection of whistleblowers. Protecting whistleblowers is an important safety measure for unearthing important public interest information.

# 2

# Towards Right to Information in India

The Right to Information (RTI) Act 2005 was enacted on 15 June 2005. The movement for right to information originated at the grass-roots level. This chapter traces the evolution of the Act.

## Right to Information as Part of the Constitution

The right to information is not explicitly stated in the Constitution. It has been the product of judicial interpretation of the Constitution by the Supreme Court. This interpretation can be viewed in the context of the Right to Freedom of Speech and Expression [Article 19(1)]. An important result of these judicial pronouncements has been that the scope of the right has gradually widened.

Restrictions were initially imposed by the Newsprint Control order of 1972–3, issued under the Essential Commodities Act 1955. Newsprint was a scarce commodity and therefore its distribution was rationed. It was challenged in *Bennet Coleman and Co. v. Union of India*, by *The Times of India*. It was contended that Newsprint Control Order imposed unreasonable restrictions on the freedom of the press. It was also argued that the restriction on the press implied restriction on the readers, who could not read newspapers of their choice. The majority judgment held that the impugned order did not merely violate the right of the newspapers to publish, which was inherent in the freedom of the press, but also violated the right of readers to information, which was included within their right to freedom of speech and expression.

In *Association for Democratic Reforms v. Union of India*, the High Court of Delhi held that voters had the right to receive relevant information about the histories of candidates who stood for elections. Indian politics has, very often, been marked by the election of individuals with legally questionable pasts. Therefore, one way of taking care of this problem is informing voters of the criminal record of the candidates. Right to information for voters is, thus, essential for healthy and transparent elections.

The court held that it is the duty of Election Commission to keep voters informed of the pasts of the candidates. It, therefore, could direct the candidates filing nominations for elections to furnish details of their assets, liabilities, past criminal cases, whether ending in acquittals or convictions, and pending criminal prosecutions. The Union Government appealed against this decision in the Supreme Court, which upheld the High Court of Delhi's decision in *Union of India v. Association for Democratic Reforms.* The Apex Court, on 2 May 2002, directed the Election Commission to demand information regarding the candidates' conviction or acquittal for any criminal offence, assets, liabilities, and educational qualifications. The Election Commission issued a directive on 28 June 2002 to this effect.

Subsequently, all political parties met on 8 July 2002 and decided that the Supreme Court judgment and the Election Commission order could not be considered pragmatic. The Government brought forth an ordinance under Article 123 of the Constitution to amend the Representation of the People Act 1951. This ordnance withdrew from the Election Commission the power to demand the required information, as mandated in the Supreme Court order. The ordinance was sent to the then-President, Dr A.P.J. Abdul Kalam, who returned it to the Parliament for reconsideration. However, since it was sent back to him thereafter, the President signed it on 24 August 2002.

The ordinance was converted into an Act and Section 33A was added. As per this section a candidate was required to give only as much information as was mentioned within the act. Demands as per the Supreme court judgment were to be ignored. Further, Section 33B, added by the Amendment Act, stated that:

> ... notwithstanding anything contained in any judgment, decree or order of any court or any direction, order or any other instruction issued by the Election Commission, no candidate shall be liable to disclose or furnish any such information, in respect of his or her election, which is not required to be disclosed or furnished under this Act or the rules made there under.

The constitutional validity of the amendment was challenged in the Supreme Court in *PUCL v. Union of*

*India.* The Supreme Court held that the amendment to the Representation of People Act, which ignored sensitive information about the candidates' pasts, violated the right to information of the voters. The logic was that the right to know the pasts of the candidates contesting election was essential for the right to freedom of speech and expression guaranteed by Article 19(1)(a) of the Constitution. The Court further stated that its decision in *Association for Democratic Reforms v. Union of India* was not mere *res judicata*—Latin term for a matter already judged—between two parties, but was a decision containing an interpretation of the Constitution. The constitutional interpretation of the Court cannot be overridden by an Act of Parliament. It requires an amendment of the Constitution. Even an amendment to the Constitution can be struck down if it violates the basic structure of the Constitution. The Government argued that the right to information was not a right included in the Constitution and has been derived by judicial interpretation. However, the Court observed that the rights which emerged through judicial interpretation of the fundamental rights were of no lesser status than the original rights mentioned in the Constitution.

## *Privilege to Withhold Documents and Right to Information*

Under Section 123 of the Indian Evidence Act, the Crown's privilege to withhold disclosure of documents was brought into Indian law, allowing the government to withhold documents which pertain to the affairs of the state, if such disclosure jeopardizes the public interest.

In *S.P. Gupta v. Union of India*, the Supreme Court examined how judges of the Supreme Court and High Courts are appointed under Article 124(2) and Article 217(1) of the Constitution, respectively. In order to determine whether requisite consultation for the appointments has taken place, it is necessary for the Court to examine the relevant papers, including correspondence between the Chief Justice of India (CJI) and the Government. On behalf of the Government, it was argued that such correspondence formed part of the advice given by the Council of Ministers and could not be disclosed by virtue of Article 74(2) of the Constitution. While dismissing this argument, the Court held that while the exact advice given by the Council of Ministers to the President could not be examined by

37

the court, the material on which such advice was based was not excluded from judicial purview.

Next, the Court dealt with the privilege to withhold the disclosure of such correspondence claimed by the Government under Section 123 read with Section 126 of the Indian Evidence Act 1872. This case was heard by a seven-judge bench, of which six held that no privilege could be claimed with respect to the documents which constituted the material for forming opinion in the case of appointment and transfer of judges.

The learned Justice P.N. Bhagwati stated, in his judgment, that there might be documents which needed to be withheld in public interest such as cabinet minutes, minutes of discussion between heads of departments, high level inter-departmental correspondence, dispatches from ambassadors from abroad, preliminary papers for submissions to be made to the cabinet, and any other document related to the framing of government policy (*Gupta*: p. 238). The need for candour and frankness must be regarded as a factor to be taken into account in determining whether, on balance, the public interest lies in favour of disclosure or against it (ibid: p. 239). Further, immunity against disclosure claimed under Section 123 of the Indian Evidence Act was not a privilege which could be waived by the state. It is an immunity which was granted in order to protect public interest. Therefore, even if the state did not claim such immunity, it was the duty of the Court to make sure that no document, the disclosure of which would harm public interest, was disclosed. The Court had to balance public interest in fair administration of justice against the public interest in the confidentiality of certain documents. Judicial discretion would be exercised so as to promote maximum openness and limit secrecy to the minimum.

The learned judge said:

Now it is obvious from the Constitution that we have adopted a democratic form of Government. Where a society has chosen to accept democracy as its creedal faith, it is elementary that the citizens ought to know what their government is doing. The citizens have a right to decide by whom and by what rules they shall be governed and they are entitled to call on those who govern on their behalf to account for their conduct. No democratic government can survive without accountability and the basic postulate of accountability is that the people should have information about functioning of the government. It is only if people know how government is functioning that they can fulfil the role which democracy assigns to them and make democracy a really effective participatory democracy.... The citizens' right to know the facts, the true facts, about the administration of the country is thus one of the pillars of a democratic state. And that is why the demand for openness in the government is increasingly growing in different parts of the world. (ibid.: p. 232)

Justice Bhagwati further said,

This is the new democratic culture of an open society towards which every liberal democracy is moving and our country should be no exception. The concept of an open government is the direct emanation from the right to know which seems to be implicit in the right of free speech and expression guaranteed under Article 19(1)(a). (ibid.: p. 232)

The Court, thus, held that where a document was withheld, a court could examine it, and only when it was convinced that its disclosure would prejudice public interest, could it allow such action. The government's privilege to withhold disclosure of documents was considered as subject to the right to information or the individual.

## Beginning of the RTI Movement in India

The real movement for right to information originated from the grass-roots level. The right to information was demanded in a similar way, as the right to work or the right to receive minimum wages. The origins of the RTI movement lie in Devdungri. This tiny place is located in central Rajasthan, about 10 kilometres south of the provincial town of Bhim, in the northern pocket of Rajasamand district that adjoins the districts of Ajmer, Bhilwara, and Pali. In 1987, four human rights activists—Nikhil Dey, Anchi, Shanker Singh, and Aruna Roy—settled in Devdungri. It is worth noting that Aruna Roy was a member of the elite Indian Administrative Service, but left it for her love to work for the people in rural areas. In the beginning, the group aimed to improve the life of the people in this economically backward region and to build an organization for the rural poor. They lived with the same facilities as those available to the ordinary small farmer in the surrounding countryside; in simple accommodations with no electricity or running water. They won the confidence of the local population due to their lifestyle, and found motivated co-workers. Devdungri soon became a meeting point for people who were concerned about social discrepancies and did not know how to confront the local elite and the officials. When their grasp in the region improved, the Mazdoor Kisan Shakti Sangathan (MKSS)—or Workers and Peasants Empowerment Organization—was founded in 1990 (Mentschel 2005: 61).

The activists initially worked in the Devdungri region, for livelihood issues which directly influenced the everyday life of the people, such as payment of lawfully guaranteed minimum wages in state development projects and drought relief programmes, as well as equitable distribution of rationed items under the public distribution system (PDS). The demand for free access to information arose in the context of minimum wages. The method of public hearings, or *Jan Sunwai*, was identified as a suitable form of voicing this right. The demand made by the MKSS, for transparency in the disbursement of all development funds, in their respective regions, was the basis of the Jan Sunwais.

The MKSS organized its first Jan Sunwai on 4 December 1994 in Kot Kirana in Pali district, followed by Bhim, Rajasamand district on 7 December 1994, in Vijaypura, Rajasamand district on 17 December 1994, in Jawaja, Ajmer district on 7 January 1995, and in Thana, Bhilwara district on 25 April 1995 (ibid.: 65). MKSS managed to get documents which pointed to irregularities in certain state development projects. The muster rolls of a number of construction projects had names of people who did not work on the construction site.

The MKSS invited local politicians, government officials, a panel of impartial observers, comprising persons from public life, human rights activists, and the press in Jan Sunwais. The direct involvement of the people differentiated the Jan Sunwai from other methods in the fight against corruption. This demonstrated the potential for collective action among groups that tend to shun organized political activity.

On 5 April 1996, the MKSS organized a *dharna* (sit-in) in the town of Beawar in Ajmer to stress the demand for the right to free access to information. The dharna became an important demonstration for the right to information. After 40 days, on 16 May, the

43

dharna of Beawar ended. The state government set up a Commission, which, within three months, had to look into the benefits and risks relating to free access to documents of the local administration. Although the Committee submitted its report on 30 August 1996, it was not made public. Further Jan Sunwais and dharnas followed (Mentschel 2005: 68–71).

The right to information became a topic for the Rajasthan Assembly elections in the second half of 1998. Ashok Gehlot, the candidate of the Congress Party for the post of the Chief Minister, supported the demands of the MKSS and included it in his election manifesto. The Congress won the election against the ruling BJP. After his election, Gehlot formed a Commission to draft a possible legislation. The State Assembly passed the Rajasthan Right to Information Act 2000 in January 1999, which came into force in June 2000.

The Rajasthan experience of demanding right to information echoed in other states. The growing demand for a right to public information from various sections of the society, led by civil society organizations in these states, could no longer be ignored.

In Maharashtra, Anna Hazare, a social activist who had practised an indigenous model of rural development in Ralegaon Siddhi, a village in Ahmednagar district near Pune, realized that development work suffered due to corruption, and the only way to combat it, was to adopt right to information legislation. In his struggle against corruption, Anna Hazare went on a fast unto death to secure the right to information law. The Maharashtra Legislative Assembly passed the Maharashtra Right to Information Act 2000, but Anna Hazare was not satisfied as the law had too many loopholes. He pressed for a new law. The Maharashtra Government had to concede that demand, and ultimately passed the Maharashtra Right to Information Act 2002. Eight states, namely Tamil Nadu, Goa, Rajastan, Karnataka, Maharashtra, Jammu and Kashmir, Assam, and Madhya Pradesh enacted laws on right to information, before the Federal Government came up with the RTI Act 2005.

## Evolution of the RTI Act 2005

It is often assumed that the RTI Act 2005 was enacted in haste. However, if one observes the legislative journey till the Act came into being, it belies that assumption.

At a national level, in 1996, a nationwide network of senior journalists, lawyers, distinguished bureaucrats, academics, and activists from non-government organizations vigorously advocated the removal of The Official Secrets Act 1923 and pushed for the legislation of the RTI Act at the centre. Other organizations which took active interest in this regard were National Campaign for Peoples' Right to Information (NCPRI) in New Delhi, Lok Satta in Andhra Pradesh, Press Council of India, and Parivartan in Delhi.

The first major draft legislation on right to information was circulated by the Press Council of India in 1996.

This was significantly based on a draft prepared earlier in a meeting of social activists, civil servants and lawyers at the Lal Bahadur Shastri National Academy of Administration, Mussoorie in October, 1995. One important feature of the Press Council draft legislation was that it affirmed in its preamble, the constitutional position that the right to information already exists under the Constitution as the natural corollary to the fundamental right to free speech and expression under

Article 19(1). It stated that the legislation merely seeks to make explicit provisions for securing to the citizen this right to information… The draft legislation affirmed the right of every citizen to information from any public body… Public body included not only State as defined in Article 12 of the Constitution but all undertakings, non-statutory authorities, company, corporation, society, trust, firm, or cooperative society owned or controlled by private individuals and institutions whose activities affect the public interest. In effect, both the corporate sector and NGOs were sought to be brought under the purview of the proposed legislation. The few restrictions that were placed on the right to information were similar to those under other Fundamental Rights… Other exemptions were bonafide grounds of individual privacy, and commercial interests… The most significant provision was that information which cannot be denied to the Parliament or the State Legislature shall not be denied to a citizen… The draft legislation laid down penalties for default in providing information in the form of fine as personal liability on the person responsible for supplying the information. (Mander and Joshi 1999)

The Government of India then constituted a Working Group on Right to Information and Transparency

47

in January 1997, under consumer activist late H.D. Shourie. The Working Group submitted the draft Bill on Freedom of Information in May 1997 and the same was circulated to all states and Union Territories for their comments. Meanwhile, a statutory scheme prepared on the basis of the deliberations of the Working Group was circulated for discussion during the Chief Ministers' Conference on 'Effective and Responsive Government', held on 24 May 1997. The statutory scheme received the broad approval of the Conference which recognized the need for the enactment of such a law.

In this context, it may be noted that the Department-related Parliamentary Standing Committee on Home Affairs (2000), in its 55th Report on the Demands for Grants (1999–2000) of the Ministry of Personnel, Public Grievances and Pensions had observed that 'the Committee in its 44th Report had recommended for the explicit provision of Right to Information... The Committee again reiterates its stand taken earlier on the matter and suggests that access to information must be accorded the status of Fundamental Right'.

The draft Freedom of Information Bill 1997, given by the Working Group and modified in light of responses of the Union ministries and ministries of the states and Union Territories was considered by the Committee of Secretaries and Cabinet. The Cabinet referred the Bill to a Group of Ministers (GoM). Accordingly, it was placed before the GoM, constituted by three successive Governments, which considered it in eight meetings held between October 1997 and February 2000. The Cabinet approved the Bill on 13 May 2000. Accordingly, the Bill was introduced in the Lok Sabha on 25 July 2000. It was referred to the Parliamentary Standing Committee on Home Affairs, chaired by Pranab Mukherjee, on 14 September 2000. The Committee considered the Bill in five sittings from October 2000 to July 2001. The Committee heard the Secretary, Ministry of Personnel, and eminent experts connected with the issue. These included renowned Indian scholars, policymakers, and analysts.

The important suggestions made by these organizations and individuals were:

(i)     The Bill should be rechristened as 'Right to Information', instead of 'Freedom of Information Bill'.
(ii)    The applicability of the Act should not be restricted only to citizens but to non-citizens as well.

(iii) The Bill should provide for a specific date from which the Act will come into effect.

(iv) The Bill should apply to all including organizations, associations, parties, trusts, unions, and societies, either private or non-governmental, in addition to government bodies and agencies.

(v) The Bill should say that all citizens 'have' the freedom of information, instead of saying 'shall have', as this freedom is already there in the Constitution.

(vi) The ultimate responsibility of ensuring adherence to the provisions of the Bill should be vested in the head of each public authority.

(vii) The Bill should clearly state that where information sought is regarding the life and liberty of a person, the same should be provided within 24 to 48 hours.

(viii) The Bill should clearly provide that all information that cannot be denied to the Members of Parliament or State Legislatures should not be denied to the public.

(ix) Section 10 of the Bill should state that reasons for withholding parts of a document must be provided to the requestor.

(x)  The period of 50 days for inviting third party representation is too long, it should be either 15 or 30 days.

(xi)  There should be a penalty for giving incorrect, incomplete, or misleading information.

(xii)  The Bill should provide for an independent appeals mechanism.

(xiii)  Provisions for providing protection to 'whistle-blowers' must be added.

(xiv)  Excluding certain organizations completely from the purview of this legislation defeats the purpose of the law. There is no rationale for exempting the administrative wings of these organizations from disclosing relevant information.

(xv)  Local bodies at grass-roots level should be included.

The Parliamentary Standing Committee felt that many of the important suggestions had not been covered in the Bill and the Government should consider incorporating them, to make it more comprehensive (Department-related Parliamentary Standing Committee on Home Affairs 2000).

The Bill was passed by the Parliament in December 2002 as the Freedom of Information (FOI) Act, and got Presidential assent on 6 January 2003. However, the Act could not be brought into force because it was not notified in the Official Gazette.

After the National Democratic Alliance (NDA) government, the United Progressive Alliance (UPA) rose to power in May 2004. The UPA agreed upon a Common Minimum Programme (CMP), which envisaged the enactment of a more progressive, participatory, and meaningful law in place of the Freedom of Information Act 2002. As per this commitment, the Government assigned the task of suggesting changes in the Act of 2002 to the National Advisory Council (NAC). The NAC, based on inputs from several NGOs, proposed around 35 amendments to the Freedom of Information Act 2002. The RTI Bill 2004 was introduced in Lok Sabha on 23 December 2004.

Some important recommendations of the NAC along with analysis of those issues in the Act of 2002 and the RTI Bill 2004 are as follows:

(i)    The Bill should prescribe a period of 120 days within which the Act would come into force. In the Act of 2002, no time limit was specified for its commencement. In the new Bill, recommendation of the NAC has been incorporated.

(ii) As in the Act of 2002, applicability of the Bill should be expanded to the state governments also. Provisions of the Bill, at present, are applicable to the central government and the bodies under its control.

(iii) Definition of 'Right to Information' should be modified so as to cover more categories. The Bill has incorporated the suggestion.

(iv) Definition of 'public authority' should be modified to cover the states, Panchayati Raj institutions, and other local bodies. The Act of 2002 has a provision of a similar nature. But the Bill restricts its applicability to the central government or bodies controlled and owned by it.

(v) Right to information should be conferred on all persons. The Bill restricts the right to citizens only.

(vi) Public Information Officers (PIOs) should be designated within one month of the enforcement of the Act. The Bill prescribes 100 days from its enactment for their appointment. The

Act of 2002 does not fix any time limit for the purpose.

(vii) Information seekers should have the liberty to request in the official language of the area, to make access procedures simple. The Act of 2002 does not provide this liberty. The Bill incorporates the suggestion.

(viii) The fee payable for seeking information should be reasonable and should not exceed actual cost of copying information. Neither the Act of 2002 nor the Bill contains any such provisions.

(ix) Information Commissioner should impose a penalty of Rs 250 for each day's delay in furnishing information. The Act of 2002 does not have penal provisions. The Bill does not empower the Information Commissioner to impose a penalty on the delinquent PIO.

The RTI Bill 2004 was referred to the Parliamentary Standing Committee on Personnel, Public Grievances, and Law and Justice, under the chairmanship of E.M. Sudarsana Natchiappan (Department-related Parliamentary Standing Committee on Personnel, Public Grievances, Law and Justice 2004).

The Parliamentary Committee heard Aruna Roy and other representatives of MKSS, NCPRI, Dr Jaiprakash, Convener, Lok Satta, and other eminent individuals like Anna Hazare, Prakash Kardaley, Maja Daruwala, Jean Dreze, Shanti Bhushan, and Shailesh Gandhi. Besides, the Committee received several written suggestions.

Their important recommendations are summarized as follows:

(i) The Bill should have a preamble to clearly state the scheme and scope of the law so that it is consistent with the principles of democracy and the ideals of the Constitution.

(ii) The applicability of the Act should not be restricted to citizens alone but should cover non-citizens as well.

(iii) The Bill should not only apply to the central government and bodies owned or controlled by it, but should be extended to the states, and other local bodies or authorities.

(iv) The information regime should be extended to the private sector.

(v) All political parties—MLAs, MPs, Ministers, and such other public representatives—should be included in the category of 'public authorities', under the Act.

(vi) There should be no provision for paying a fee at the time of making a request for information.

(vii) The fee charged under clause 7(5) must be reasonable, affordable, and should, in no case, exceed the actual cost of supplying the information. There should be a provision for waiving the fee in case the information is in larger public interest.

(viii) The exemptions should be justified by a strong risk to public interest, in the sense that citizens should have access to information about the agencies, their policies, personnel, and so on, so far as the information relates to corruption and issues of public interest.

(ix) Clause 11 of the Bill lays down procedure for seeking third party information. This clause, by its nature, provides the PIO and the third party an opportunity to deny information on the ground of confidentiality. It should, therefore, be deleted.

(x)   To ensure that the Commission and its functionaries perform their duties independently and with autonomy, the Information Commissioner and the Deputy Information Commissioners should be given the status of the Chief Election Commissioner and the Election Commissioner respectively.

(xi)  There should be a provision clarifying that the Information Commissioner can hear an appeal where an applicant has received no response to an appeal, under sub-clause (1) of clause 16.

The Parliamentary Standing Committee asked the Government to consider these suggestions. It also recommended that people living below poverty line (BPL) should be exempted from paying any fee for accessing information, and, in other cases, it should not exceed the actual cost of supplying the information. Further, the Parliamentary Committee recommended bringing the states and other local bodies or authorities within the purview of the proposed RTI Bill and other consequential changes like the constitution of the State Information Commission.

The final report of the Standing Committee was presented to the Rajya Sabha on 21 March 2004 and tabled in the Lok Sabha on same day. The Bill was passed by both Houses of Parliament in May 2005. It received the assent of the President on 15 June 2005 and was published in The Gazette of India on 21 June 2005.

## *Status of State Acts after Enactment of the Central RTI Act 2005*

Since the RTI Act 2005, passed by the Parliament, does not repeal any of the state laws on that subject, but repeals only the Freedom of Information Act 2002, both the central law, that is, RTI Act 2005, and the state law will operate within each state which has passed the law. However, in the state of Jammu and Kashmir, only the state law, the Jammu and Kashmir Right to Information Act 2009, which is closely based upon the central RTI Act 2005, will operate.

In other states where RTI laws exist, the citizens have a choice between the two laws in force simultaneously, while seeking information from the state government and its public bodies. However, most state laws are weaker than the national law.

It is suggested that to avoid confusion, the state governments should repeal their laws and adopt the central law. Also, a uniform law on access to information for the entire country will make it more effective.

# 3

# Right to Information Act 2005

## Overview of the RTI Act 2005

The Right to Information Act 2005 applies to whole of India except the state of Jammu and Kashmir. Jammu and Kashmir has enacted the Jammu and Kashmir Right to Information Act 2009, repealing and replacing the erstwhile Jammu and Kashmir Right to Information Act 2004 and Jammu and Kashmir Right to Information (Amendment) Act 2008. This Act is closely based on the Central RTI Act 2005 wherein the people of the state can seek information from the state government under the state Act, and can also use the Central RTI Act 2005 to acquire information from the central government public authorities. With the enactment of the central law, some states have repealed their laws. Where the state Act has not been repealed, both the central and state Acts will operate simultaneously. In case of conflict, the central law will prevail.

The RTI Act 2005 aims to strike a balance between extending people's access to official information and preserving confidentiality where disclosure would be against public interest. What goes without saying, however, is that information is available unless it falls under a specified exemption.

The main features of the Act are:

1. All *citizens* have right to information.

Section 3

2. The Act defines *information* in very broad manner. It includes any material in any form, including records, documents, memos, e-mails, opinions, advice, press releases, circulars, orders, logbooks, contracts, reports, papers, samples, models, data material held in any electronic form, and information relating to any private body which can be accessed by a public authority under any other law for the time being in force.

Section 2(f)

3. The Act defines *record* as:

    (i)     any document, manuscript, or file;

    (ii)    any microfilm, microfiche, or facsimile copy of a document;

    (iii)   any reproduction of image or images, embodied in such microfilm (whether enlarged or not); and

    (iv)    any other material produced by a computer or any other device.

    Section 2(i)

4. Right to information means the right to information *accessible* under this act, which is held by or under the control of any public authority and includes the right to:

    (i)     inspect work, documents, or records;

    (ii)    take notes, extracts, or certified copies of documents or records;

    (iii)   take certified samples of material; and

    (iv)    obtain information in the form of diskettes, floppies, tapes, video cassettes, or in any other electronic mode or through printouts where such information is stored in a computer or in any other device.

    Section 2(j)

5.  Public authority means any authority or body or institution of self-government established or constituted:

    (i)    by or under the Constitution;

    (ii)   by any other law made by the Parliament;

    (iii)  by any other law made by the State Legislature; and

    (iv)   by notification issued or order made by the appropriate Government and includes any

           (a) body owned, controlled, or substantially financed;

           (b) non-government organization substantially financed directly or indrectly by funds provided by appropriate Government.

                                            Section 2(h)

6.  Advocates *proactive disclosure* by public authorities.

                                            Section 4

7.  Lays down implementation mechanism by way of appointment of Public Information Officers (PIOs), Appellate officers in all public authorities, while stipulating time limit for disposing request for information and setting up of Information Commissions in centre and states.

                             Sections 5, 6, 7, and 12 to 17

8. It prescribes *the process for obtaining information and disposal of requests*. The application under RTI can be submitted in writing or electronically in English or Hindi or in the official language of the area in which the application is being made, with a prescribed fee, to the PIO or Assistant Public Information Officer (APIO) [Section 6(1)].

   Information is to be provided within 30 days or 48 hours where life or liberty is involved [Section 7(1)]. The period can extend to 35 days where request is given to APIO [Section 5(2)]. However, the time taken for intimation and payment of fees is excluded from the above time frame [Section 7(3)(a)]. If no action is taken on the application within the stipulated time, it is deemed as a refusal [Section 7(2)].

9. It constructs two-tier mechanism for appeal. The first appeal is made to an officer within the organization, who is senior in rank to the PIO. The second appeal is made to the Information Commission.

   Section 19(1) and Section 19(3)

10. It specifies the information which can be exempted from disclosure:

(i)     Information which would prejudicially affect the sovereignty and integrity of India, the security, strategic, scientific or economic interests of the state, relation with foreign state or lead to incitement of an offence;

Section 8(1)(a)

(ii)    Information which has been expressly forbidden to be published by any court of law or tribunal or the disclosure of which may constitute contempt of court;

Section 8(1)(b)

(iii)   Information, the disclosure of which, would cause a breach of privilege of Parliament or the State Legislature;

Section 8(1)(c)

(iv)    Information including commercial confidence, trade secrets or intellectual property, the disclosure of which would harm the competitive position of a third party, unless the competent authority is satisfied that larger public interest warrants the disclosure;

Section 8(1)(d)

(v)     Information available to a person in his fiduciary relationship, unless the competent authority is satisfied that the larger public interest warrants the disclosure of such information;

Section 8(1)(e)

(vi) Information received in confidence from a foreign government;

Section 8(1)(f)

(vii) Information, the disclosure of which, would endanger the life or physical safety of any person or identify the source of information or assistance given in confidence for law enforcement or security purposes;

Section 8(1)(g)

(viii) Information which would impede the process of investigation, apprehension, or prosecution of offenders;

Section 8(1)(h)

(ix) Cabinet papers, including records of deliberations of the Council of Ministers, Secretaries, and other officers;

Provided that the decisions of the Council of Ministers, the reasons for those decisions, and the material on the basis of which the decisions were made shall be made public after the decision has been taken, and the matter is complete, or over;

Provided, further, that those matters which come under the exemptions specified in this section shall not be disclosed;

Section 8(1)(i)

(x)    Information which relates to personal information, the disclosure of which, has no relationship to any public activity or interest, or which would cause unwarranted invasion of the privacy of the individual unless larger public interest justifies the disclosure;

Section 8(1)(j)

(xi)    The information which cannot be denied to the Parliament or a State Legislature shall not be denied to any person.

Proviso to Section 8(1)

(xii)    Notwithstanding anything in the Official Secrets Act 1923, nor any of the exemptions permissible in accordance with Section 8(1), a *public authority may allow access to information, if public interest in disclosure outweighs the harm to the protected interests.*

Section 8(2)

(xiii) Information can be denied if it would involve infringement of copyright subsisting in a person other than the state. (This is the only absolute exemption in the Act.)

Section 9

(xiv) The Act will not apply to the intelligence and security organizations specified in the Second Schedule of the Act, but information pertaining to allegations of corruption and human rights violations is to be provided all the same. However, information regarding allegations of violation of human rights shall be provided after the approval of the Information Commission.

Section 24

(xv) Third party information to be released after giving notice to, and hearing off, the third party.

Section 11

(xvi) Where a request for access to information is rejected due to it being exempt from disclosure, then, notwithstanding any clause contained in the Act, access may be provided to that part of the record which does not contain any of the exempt information and which can reasonably be severed.

Section 10(1)

(xvii) Information Commissions to receive and inquire into a complaint, and to act as second appellate authority. The Commission has the same powers as vested in civil court while trying a civil suit under the Code of Civil Procedure 1908. It can impose a penalty, and in case of persistent failure, recommend disciplinary action against the PIO.

Sections 18, 19, 20

(xviii) The Act's provisions shall have effect notwithstanding anything inconsistent with the Official Secrets Act 1923 or any other law. No court can entertain any suit regarding any order made under this Act other than by way of an appeal under this Act.

Sections 22, 23

(xix) One unique aspect of the Act is that it is wholly retrospective. It does not apply only to information created or held by public authorities after it has come into force. It applies to all information held by public authorities regardless of date.

## How the RTI Act has Helped: Success Stories

Although much has to be done, particularly in the rural areas, there have been numerous cases where the citizens have received what is due to them thanks to the RTI Act. There can be various kinds of impacts of RTI, such as preventing corruption, exposing corruption, curtailing wasteful public expenditure, exposing misuse of power and influence, accessing justice, redressing grievances, and so on. Civil society organizations and the news media have played an active role in enhancing the reach and awareness of right to information among the masses. It is mostly with the support of social activists and civil society organizations that a person living in a village is able to use the RTI Act.

The Corruption Perception Index brought out by Transparency International for the year 2010 ranked India 87th out of 178 countries. Broadly, there are two types of corruption. First, there is big ticket corruption associated with abuse of discretion in allocation of resources, and the second is petty corruption, which we often see in our day-to-day interaction with government. In recent times, there appears to be a decline in petty corruption, but there is increased big ticket corruption as evident from major scandals, such as 2G, Commonwealth Games, and the Adarsh Housing Society scandal. Use of RTI has helped expose many scams.

A recent report by the Centre for Media Studies (CMS) indicates that the percentage of rural households which paid bribes has come down from 56 per cent to 28 per cent between 2005 and 2010. However, in the public distribution system (PDS), the percentage of rural households paying bribes mainly for getting a ration card almost tripled (CMS 2010).

Two Yale University researchers, Leonid Peisakhin and Paul Pinto, conducted an experiment on slum dwellers in Delhi, who applied for a ration card. The applicants were randomly assigned to one of the four experimental groups. The first group applied for a ration card and then did nothing about it, the second group attached a letter of recommendation from an

NGO to their application, the third paid a bribe after putting in their application, and the fourth enquired about the status of their ration card application through a right to information request shortly after the initial application. It was found that although the group that paid bribes was by far the most successful in getting their application processed faster, the group that put in an RTI request was almost as successful (Peisakhin and Pinto 2010).

By the use of this Act, one can determine the services, rights, and benefits one is entitled to. However, the use of the RTI Act is not a solution in itself. It is a first step and on receipt of the information, one can file a complaint and ask for an Action Taken Report on it. For example, using the RTI Act may not get applicants electricity or water, but it can help them find out the person responsible for their application. They can determine the extent of progress, time frame for the connection, and reasons for delay in the particular case. It is generally seen, that in many instances, the use of RTI itself has helped the citizens in solving the issues which have otherwise remained unattended for fairly long period. It has been seen that unserviceable roads, non-clearance of garbage, misuse of government funds, delay in clearing of cases, maintenance of street lights, public parks, and so on, have been put right just by filing an RTI application. The very thought of answering citizens and exposing their inefficiencies has put fear in the minds of public functionaries.

There are a number of success stories where people have been empowered by the use of the RTI Act. It has resulted in their acquiring what they are entitled to, like ration card, food entitlement, pension, housing, electricity connection, and so on. Numerous cases are there where RTI Act has been helpful in exposing corrupt practices (Daruwala and Nayak 2008: 67–8). Poorest Areas Civil Society (PACS) brought out a publication, *Action Research Villages: A Right to Information Campaign*, which brings out a number of success stories regarding RTI campaigns in the remote villages of India, where the local populace fought for their rights and got justice. *Action Village Research* is a testimony to the fact that a little spark of knowledge can ignite a people's campaign. This may turn into a mass movement to provide justice to the common man through the right to information (Sharma et al. 2007).

# Assessing Impact of the RTI Act 2005

## *PRIA Study*

To assess the impact of the RTI Act, a study on its working in 12 states was conducted in August 2006, by the Society for Participatory Research in Asia (PRIA).

The study found that self-disclosure at district, block, and panchayat levels has not started in the 12 states. Also, nearly 90 per cent of people are not aware of the Act and cannot file the applications. Use of RTI is restricted to educated sections, particularly government servants. Further, the government has not undertaken any campaign for making RTI popular among people.

## *Study by Pragati Abhiyan*

A study was conducted by the Pragati Abhiyan, a civil society organization working on rural develop-ment issues during December 2007 in 84 offices of the government in Nashik district (Kulkarni 2008). These offices were spread across Nashik city, Igatpuri, Traimbakeshwar, and Peth tehsils. The focus of study was whether these offices were complying with the mandatory requirement of proactive disclosure under Section 4 of the Act. Applications were also filed with the District Supply Officer of Nashik district to get information about the number of ration card holders of various categories, like below poverty line (BPL), Antyodaya, above poverty line, and so on. The Antyodaya Anna Yojana Scheme, for example, was launched by the government in 2000 to provide special food-based assistance to destitute households. These households are given a special ration card (an 'Antyodaya card') which entitles them to get wheat and rice at Rs 2 and Rs 3 per kilogram, respectively. Also, information was sought about the monthly quota allotments, the monthly lifting of PDS supplies and the total monthly sales at tehsil level for the year 2007. An application was also made to the Deputy Collector in-charge of the Employment Guarantee Scheme (EGS) for Nashik district, asking for village-wise information about EGS-related work done in four tehsils of Nashik.

The chief finding of this study was that many government offices still do not have a PIO and rarely comply with Section 4 of the Act. Further, while information exists in the raw form, it is generally not kept in a consolidated format. The information asked for is of importance to administrators of the scheme at the district or state level, yet its absence in the offices of decision-making authorities suggests the absence of monitoring.

## *Commonwealth Human Rights Initiative (CHRI) Study*

In 2009, the Commonwealth Human Rights Initiative (CHRI) and Nagarik Adhikar Kendra, Kalol conducted a survey to assess compliance of public authorities with their obligations, under the RTI Act, in Panchmahals district in state of Gujarat (CHRI 2009). This district was selected by the state government in 2006–7 for intensive capacity building of public authorities under the UNDP sponsored programme. The major findings of the survey were that the first bottleneck encountered by a citizen visiting a public office is 'who do I contact for information?' At taluka level, less than 20 per cent of the offices displayed notice boards containing the name of the PIO and Appellate Authorities. Regarding availability and accessibility of proactively disclosed information as required under Section 4(1)

(b) of the RTI Act, less than 40 per cent of the offices at taluka level confirmed that they had compiled this information. Only 61 per cent of taluka offices had maintained data about receipt and disposal of RTI applications. The performance of district level offices was better on these counts.

## *PricewaterhouseCoopers (PwC) Study*

An extensive study was carried out for assessing and evaluating the RTI Act with focus on the key issues and constraints faced by 'Information Providers' and 'Information Seekers', by PricewaterhouseCoopers (PwC 2009). The initiative was taken by the Department of Personnel and Training (DoPT), Government of India. The five states were selected on the basis of population, literacy level, per capita income, proportion of disadvantaged population, and urban population as a percentage of total population. These five states were Uttar Pradesh, Maharashtra, Andhra Pradesh, Orissa, and Assam.

The study takes into account the feedbacks of over 2,000 information seekers and over 200 information providers, across public authorities at the centre, state, and local levels. It also included the feedbacks of 5,000 citizens with respect to their awareness of the RTI Act. The key findings were:

1. Only 13 per cent of the rural population and 33 per cent in urban population were aware of the RTI Act.

2. Only 12 per cent of women and 26 per cent of men were aware of the RTI Act.

3. More than 33 per cent of the respondents surveyed complained of multiple visits to the public authority office for filing an RTI application.

4. Economic cost of filing an RTI application was estimated at Rs 460–510 in urban areas and Rs 230–70 in rural areas. This includes the cost of repeated visits (on an average 1.96 visits) and lost wages (assumed to be minimum wages).

5. 54 per cent of the respondents surveyed complained of apathetic attitude of PIOs.

6. 77 per cent of the central PIO were not aware of Proactive Disclosures.

7. None of the public authorities in surveyed states made an effort to capture information needs and reflect them in their Proactive Disclosure.

8. Central and state schemes do not contain RTI-specific guidelines for proactive information disclosure.
9. Guidelines for Information providers and seekers have not been widely disseminated.
10. Record Management System was cited as the major reason for delay in processing of RTI application (above 80 per cent in Andhra Pradesh, Assam, and Maharashtra).
11. 46 per cent of the PIOs at central level, 72 per cent of the PIOs in Assam, and 50 per cent of the PIOs in Andhra Pradesh have not received training.

## RTI Assessment and Analysis Group (RaaG) and National Campaign for People's Right to Information (NCPRI) Report of the People's RTI Assessment

The report (RaaG 2009) was based on interviews with 37,704 people and visits to 1,027 public authorities in rural, district, state, and central level in ten states and Delhi. The RTI applicants included economically weaker sections of people to the extent of about 30 per cent in rural and 15 per cent in urban areas.

The major findings were as follows:

1.  There is poor awareness about the RTI Act, especially in the rural areas.
2.  Less than half the PIOs and an even lesser proportion of other civil servants have been oriented and trained towards facilitating the right to information.
3.  All state and Union Territory Governments, all the High Courts and Legislative assemblies, the central government, the Supreme Court, and both houses of Parliament have a right to make their own rules and procedures. There is a need to develop consensus on a common set of rules.
4.  Applicants, especially from the weaker segments of society, are often intimidated, threatened, and even physically attacked when they go to submit an RTI application, or as a consequence of their submitting such an application. Over 40 per cent of rural applicants stated that the most important constraint they faced in exercising their right to information was harassment and threats from officials.
5.  Despite Section 4 of the RTI Act, there is poor compliance by public authorities.

6.  Information Commission orders are of varying quality, often with poor consistency on similar issues across Commissions, within Commissions, and even among the orders of the same Commissioner.
7.  The mechanism for monitoring the implementation of the RTI Act, and for receiving and assimilating feedback, is almost non-existent.

## Initiatives for Effective Implementation of the RTI Act

Some states, notably Bihar and Andhra Pradesh, have taken a number of initiatives in implementing the Act.

### *Bihar* 'Jaankari': *Right to Information Call Centre*

Bihar was the first State in the country to create a Right to Information Call Centre: 'Jaankari'. The applicant has to dial 155311 for filing an application under RTI Act 2005. She has to provide her name and address for communication. The call centre executive drafts the application on the basis of the taped phone call. The onus of identifying the right public authority and sending the application there is on the call centre. An application fee of Rs 10 is credited in the telephone bill. Once the application has been filed and entered into the system, a copy is sent to the applicant and another to the concerned PIO. The information can be obtained in Hindi, English, Maithili, or Bhojpuri. Information is sent directly to the applicant. First and second appeal processes are also carried out, following a similar pattern.

## *Andhra Pradesh*

In Andhra Pradesh, citizens who have pending appeals or complaints with the Andhra Pradesh Information Commission (APIC) can determine the status of such appeals/complaints by sending an SMS to APIC on a particular mobile phone number, citing the appeal number and the year. A reply SMS indicating the status of the appeal/complaint is sent. This has been achieved with the help of Centre for Good Governance, Hyderabad.

Further, the following innovative steps have been taken:

(i) Introduced an elaborate system of compiling RTI data from various public authorities. This facilitates the Government to monitor the implementation of the Act.

(ii) High-level Monitoring Committee, headed by the Chief Secretary on RTI matters in the state, meets once in a quarter.

(iii) The following initiatives for awareness generation about RTI were taken:

    (a) Preparation of slides for exhibition in cinema theatres and beaming of strips on TV channels;

    (b) Preparation of short films for telecasting on TV or cinema halls;

    (c) Display of information on boards and presentation of templates in rural areas;

    (d) Preparation of e-learning module on RTI, under the technical support of the Centre for Good Governance, Hyderabad.

Further, to propagate RTI Act at grass-roots level, the Government has incorporated RTI lessons in school education, where it is taught through interesting narratives, in dialogue form, followed by questions and activities to be taken up by children.

The Union Government issued a letter to the Chief Secretaries of all states (except the state of Jammu and Kashmir) and Union Territories to take similar actions in their states.

## Union Government Guidelines for Strengthening Implementation of the RTI Act

The Government of India asked all Ministries/ Departments/Attached Offices/PSUs of the central government to take the following actions:

(a) In the Annual reports from the year 2011–12 onwards, a separate chapter shall be included regarding the implementation of the RTI Act in their respective offices. This chapter should detail the number of RTI applications received and disposed off during the year, including number of cases in which information was denied.

(b) Each Ministry/Department should organize at least a half day training programme for all Central

Public Information Officers (CPIOs)/Appellate Authorities (AAs) every year, to sensitize them about their role in the implementation of the RTI Act. Similar programs should be conducted for all CPIOs/AAs of all attached/subordinate offices and PSUs.

(c) All public authorities who have a website shall publish the details of monthly receipts and disposals of RTI applications on the website. This should be implemented within 10 days of the close of the month. Monthly reporting on the above pattern should begin latest by 10 July 2011 for the month of June 2011 and thereafter should continue on a regular basis.

## Issues in Implementation of the RTI Act 2005

The PwC report on understanding the 'Key Issues and Constraints in implementing the RTI Act', in June 2009, brought out the issues faced by Information Seekers and Information Suppliers—PIOs and public authorities—as under:

Issues faced by Information Seekers, inter-alia, involves:

(a) Awareness about RTI in rural population among women, and disadvantaged sections of society— OBC/SC/ST—is low.

(b) Constraints in filing RTI applications, which are due to:

    (i)    non-availability of User Guides;

    (ii)   absence of signage for locating the concerned public PIO at a public authority;

    (iii)  multiple visits to the PIO's office for submission of RTI application; and

    (iv)  non-friendly attitude of the PIOs.

(c) More than 75 per cent of citizens were dissatisfied with the quality of information being provided.

Issues faced by the PIOs and public authorities are:

(a) Failure to provide information within stipulated time due to inadequate record management and absence of enabling infrastructure like computers, scanners, photocopiers, and internet connectivity.

(b) Inadequate number of trained PIOs and Appellate Authorities. The survey revealed that only 55 per cent of surveyed PIOs had received RTI training.

(c) Lack of motivation among PIOs as this job was only an additional responsibility without corresponding incentive.

(d) Absence of adequate mechanisms within public authorities to implement the provisions of the Act, like suo moto disclosure.

On the positive side, the survey revealed that over 20 per cent of rural and 45 per cent of urban PIOs claimed that changes had been made in the functioning of their offices, because of RTI. Over 60 per cent of these changes pertained to improving record maintenance, but interestingly, in 10 per cent of rural public authorities and 25 per cent of urban ones, resulting changes were in procedures of functioning and decision-making.

### *Large Pendency of Cases before Information Commissions*

Another issue is the large number of pending appeals/ complaints before Information Commissions. There were 26,049 cases pending before CIC as on December 2011. It has been estimated by the author that from the year 2007 to 2011, the average number of monthly receipts was 856, 1214, 1792, 2299, and 2748, respectively. Corresponding to this, average monthly disposal has been 581, 857, 1636, 1964, and 1868, respectively. The Commission is working only at about half its sanctioned strength, but the disposal of cases has considerably improved, barring year 2011.

# 4

# Right of Information Seekers

## Who is Eligible to Seek Information?

All citizens of India have the right to information under Section 3 of the Right to Information (RTI) Act. During the discussion of the Freedom of Information (FOI) Bill 2000 and the RTI Bill 2004 many favoured extending this right to all persons. However, as the fundamental rights in the Constitution are exercisable by citizens alone, the Parliamentary Committee recommended it for the same.

An office-bearer of an Association or Union can also make use of the RTI Act and as long as the information seeker is a citizen of India, it does not matter whether he or she is also an office-bearer of an organization. However, if an RTI application is filed by a company or a firm and is signed by the authorized representative of the firm, then such application is not maintainable.

Some important cases decided by the Central Information Commission (CIC) in this regard, are discussed in the following sections.

In *Sreekumar S. Menon, General Secretary, Kerala Peoples' Forum v. Indian Audit and Accounts Department, Kerala,* the appellant was refused information by the Central Public Information Officer (CPIO) as the request was under the name of the Kerala Peoples' Forum. The Commission held that Section 3 of the RTI Act, which gives the right to citizens of India, has to be liberally interpreted. So long as the information seeker is an identifiable person who is a citizen of India, it should matter little whether or not he is also office bearer of an organization. The fact that the information seeker is a citizen, entitles him to information under the RTI Act. It could not have been the intention of the legislature, that while entitling the citizens alone for information under the RTI Act, all those citizens who happen to be office-bearers of organizations will stand excluded from the benefits of the Act. Therefore, even if information is sought by an office bearer of an

Association or Union, the same should be treated as valid in terms of the RTI Act, provided it is made in their capacity as a citizen.

In *The Secretary, the Cuttack Tax Bar Association, Cuttack v. The Commissioner of Income Tax, Cuttack, Orissa,* the issue was whether Section 3 of the RTI Act entitles an association of citizens to receive information. The main contention of the appellant was that Section 3 of the RTI Act is merely declaratory in nature and does not vest any right on anyone to information. It does not explicitly declare who can apply for information. It simply declares that all citizens shall have the right to information. It is Section 6(1) of the RTI Act which states who is entitled to apply for information. Since Section 6(1) entitles every person to apply for any information, every person is, therefore, so entitled. The appellants further argued that the term 'person' is not defined in the RTI Act and hence the definition given in Section 3(42) of the General Clauses Act 1897 has to be applied. According to this Section, a 'person shall include any company or association or body of individuals, whether incorporated or not'. The appellants cited a number of decisions of the Apex Court where 'person' also included juristic persons.

The Full Bench of the Commission stated that one has to bear in mind that the RTI Act confers this right not on all 'persons' but only on 'citizens', and there is no ambiguity about the definition of the term 'citizen'. A juristic person can be a person but he cannot be a citizen. Every citizen is a person but the reverse is not true. An artificial or juristic person cannot be a citizen. The Commission stated that the appellant's argument that Section 3 of the RTI Act is merely a declaratory provision and it is Section 6(1) of the RTI Act which confers the relevant right is, untenable. Section 3 of the RTI Act is the leading provision; Section 6(1) deals with a procedural aspect and has, therefore, to be regarded as a subordinate provision.

The Commission observed that the application under the RTI Act was submitted in the name of the Association and was signed by the Secretary, whose name as an individual can be ascertained only from the Letter head of the Association and his signature, *per se*, does not signify the identity of the signatory. The first and second appeals have been filed not in the name of an individual citizen, but by the Secretary, Cuttack Bar Association thus leaving no doubt that it is the Association which is the applicant and the appellant is a distinct legal entity. The Association or its Secretary in its official designation cannot be treated as 'citizen' under the law.

## Rights Conferred on Citizens under the Act

The rights conferred on citizens under the RTI Act 2005 include:

1.  The right to information

    Section 3
2.  Choosing medium of request (in writing or through electronic means) for obtaining Information

    Section 6(1)
3.  Choosing language of request (in English or Hindi or in the official language of the area in which the application is made) for obtaining information

    Section 6(1)
4.  Seeking help in writing request Proviso to Section 6(1)
5.  Not stating any reason for requesting Information or providing any other personal details except those necessary for contacting the applicant

    Section 6(2)

6.  If request for information is transferred to another public authority, to be informed immediately about such transfer

    Section 6(3)

7.  Right with respect to review the decision about amount of fees charged, or the form of access provided

    Section 7(3)(b)

8.  Assistance in accessing record, if applicant is disabled

    Section 7(4)

9.  All fees are waived for below poverty line (BPL) applicants

    Section 7(5)]

10. All fees are waived if a public authority fails to supply information within the specified time limits

    Section 7(6)

11. Knowledge of reasons for rejection, period within which an appeal can be made, and particulars of appellate authority (AA)

    Section 7(8)

12. Making of complaint to CIC/SIC, as the case may be if:

    (a)    Unable to submit request to PIO/APIO

    Section 18(1)(a)

(b) Refused access to information

Section 18(1)(b)

(c) Not given response within time limit

Section 18(1)(c)

(d) Required to pay unreasonable fee

Section 18(1)(d)

(e) Provided incomplete, misleading information or false information

Section 18(1)(e)

(f) In respect of any matter relating to accessing record

Section 18(1)(f)

13. Can prefer an appeal

Section 19(1) and Section 19(3)

## What Sort of 'Information' can be Sought?

The Act defines '*Information*' in a very broad manner. It includes '*any material in any form*, including records, documents, memos, e-mails, opinions, advice press releases, circulars, orders, logbooks, contracts, reports, papers, samples, models, data material held in any electronic form, *and information relating to any private body*

95

*which can be accessed by a public authority under any other law for the time being in force.'* [Section 2 (f)]

Information available with the public authority falls under Section 2(f) of the RTI Act. The last part of Section 2(f),

> ... information relating to any private body which can be accessed by a public authority under any other law for the time being in force' broadens the scope of the term 'information' to include information which is not available, but can be accessed by the public authority from a private authority. Such information relating to a private body should be accessible to the public authority under any other law.

Therefore, Section 2(f) of the RTI Act requires examination of the relevant statute or law under which a public authority can access information from a private body. If a law or statute permits and allows the public authority to access the information relating to a private body, it will falls under the purview of Section 2(f) of the RTI Act. If there are preconditions and restrictions to be satisfied by the public authority before information can be accessed, and a private body asked to furnish it, then such preconditions and restrictions have to be fulfilled. This was evident in *Poorna Prajna Public School v. CIC and Others.*

The words 'opinions' and 'advices' in Section 2(f) only mean opinion and advice obtained by a public authority in a given matter from any agency, department, persons, and so on, forming part of the file (see, for example, *Aakash Aggarwal v. Debts Recovery Tribunal, New Delhi*). These words cannot be construed to mean that any citizen can solicit from the CPIO or the latter's opinion on any given matter.

The scope of 'information' is given in the definition of *'right to information'* under Section 2(j), which includes the right to:

(i)    inspection of work, documents, and records;
(ii)   taking notes, extracts, or certified copies of documents or records;
(iii)  taking certified samples of material; and
(iv)   obtaining information in the form of diskettes, floppies, tapes, video cassettes, or in any other electronic mode or through printouts where such information is stored in a computer or in any other device.

A citizen can thus ask for physical inspection of the construction of a road, or installation of a hand pump, and so on. One can examine files, get notes, certified copies of documents/records, and samples of material. A citizen can ask for a sample of road being built to check whether appropriate materials have been used as specified in the contract. Right to information includes taking certified samples of material but does not include asking the public authority to get it tested. One such example is *B.P. Srivastava, Editor, Sub Ki Khabar, Delhi v. Executive Engineer, PWD*. Also, videography of records/samples is permitted at one's own expense (see *Sanjay Singh v. PWD*).

In *Central Board of Secondary Education and Anr v. Aditya Bandopadhyay,* the Supreme Court held:

> At this juncture, it is necessary to clear some misconceptions about the RTI Act. The RTI Act provides access to all information that is available and existing. This is clear from a combined reading of section 3 and the definitions of 'information' and 'right to information' under clauses (f) and (j) of section 2 of the Act. If a public authority has any information in the form of data or analysed data, or abstracts, or statistics, an applicant may access such information, subject to the

exemptions in section 8 of the Act. But where the information sought is not a part of the record of a public authority, the Act does not cast an obligation upon the public authority, to collect or collate such non-available information and then furnish it to an applicant. A public authority is also not required to furnish information which require drawing of inferences and/or making of assumptions. It is also not required to provide 'advice' or 'opinion' to an applicant, nor required to obtain and furnish any 'opinion' or 'advice' to an applicant. The reference to 'opinion' or 'advice' in the definition of 'information' in section 2(f) of the Act, only refers to such material available in the records of the public authority. Many public authorities have, as a public relation exercise, provide advice, guidance and opinion to the citizens. But that is purely voluntary and should not be confused with any obligation under the RTI Act.

Further, in *Dr. Celsa Pinto v. Goa State Information Commission*, the High Court of Bombay at Goa ruled that:

> ... the definition of information cannot include within its fold answers to the question 'why' which would be same thing as asking the reason for a justification

for a particular thing. The public information authorities cannot expect to communicate to the citizen the reason why a certain thing was done or not done in the sense of justification because the citizen makes a requisition about information. Justifications are matter within the domain of adjudicating authorities and cannot properly be classified as information.

## *Provisions Regarding Disclosure of File Notings*

It is interesting to note that on 15 June 2005, the day the President gave assent to the RTI Act 2005, he wrote to the Prime Minister:

4. The definition of the words, 'information' in Section 2(f); 'record' in Section 2(i) and 'right to information' in Section 2(j) are such that even note portions of the file which contain advice/opinion tendered by officials on arriving at a final decision can be insisted upon for production. This is not a fair approach and will harm the process of decision making as officials would be more cautious in or even refrain from rendering objective, frank and written advise on file. Sharing of information on decisions taken and sharing of information on how the decision is actually arrived

at have entirely different diamensions and ought to have been handled differently. (Singh 2011: 83–4)

The Prime Minister responded to the President on 26 July 2005:

14. You have very correctly pointed out that 'note' portion of files should not be disclosed to the citizens, who invoke the provisions of this Act. I fully agree that the notings contain the deliberations inside a department or across departments, preceding a decision. The disclosure of 'note' portion of a file will inhibit civil servants, experts and advisors from recording their views freely and frankly.

15. I may share with you that the draft of the RTI Bill, which was received from the National Advisory Council for consideration of the Government, had mentioned file notings as one of the items that can be disclosed. But the Group of Ministers, as well as the Department-related Parliamentary Standing Committee, pointedly excluded file notings from the items liable for disclosure.

16. As you well aware, it is the practice in Government that file notings are withheld even when they are summoned by courts of law. Accordingly, file notings may also be excluded from disclosure

requirement under this Act. As you have pointed out, it may be possible for someone to seek disclosure of file notings under such expression as 'records', 'advice', 'memo' and so on. In case it is noticed that file notings are in danger of exposure under this Act, we will consider amending the Act suitably at the appropriate time. (ibid.: 85–9)

In this connection, there is also a communication between the Prime Minister and Anna Hazare, wherein the Prime Minister wrote:

File notings were never covered in the definition of 'information' in the RTI Act passed by Parliament. In fact, the amendments being currently proposed expand the scope of the Act to specifically include file notings relating to development and social issues. The overall effort is to promote even greater transparency and accountability in our decision making process. (ibid.: 90)

Soon after the RTI Act became operative, Department of Personnel and Training (DoPT), the department of the Government of India central to RTI declared on its website that file notings need not be disclosed. This was challenged and various information commissioners held that file notings are disclosable under the Act. The Government tried to amend the Act but abstained due to civil society pressure.

In a number of cases, the CIC had directed the DoPT to remove from its website 'information' that did not include the file notings. Finally, in *Subhash Chandra Agrawal v. DoPT*, the Commission directed the Joint Secretary (AT&T) and Deputy Secretary (RTI) to appear before it on 17 June 2009 to show cause for disobeying its orders and thus committing offences punishable under Sections 166,187, and 188 of Indian Penal Code.

Thereafter, the nodal department issued orders on 23 June 2009 that file notings are disclosable, except those containing information exempt from disclosure under Section 8 of the Act.

In *Dr. R.K. Garg v. Ministry of Home Affairs,* the Commission observed that confidential file notings by one officer were meant for the next officer with whom he may be in a hierarchical relationship. It is in the nature of a fiduciary entrustment, and it should not ordinarily be disclosed, surely not without the concurrence of the officer preparing that note. When read together, Section 11(1) and Section 8(1)(e) unerringly point to a conclusion that notings of a 'confidential' file should be disclosed only after giving opportunity to the third party, such as, the officer(s) writing those notes, to be heard.

## Information Exempted from Disclosure

Though the RTI Act gives citizens access to a broad range of information, there are provisions where some information is exempted from disclosure. There are 10 exemptions under Section 8(1). These have been exhaustively dealt in the Chapter 6.

These exemptions are not absolute. If the information sought is covered by an exemption, but public interest in disclosure outweighs the harm the exemptions are protecting, then it can still be released. This is known as the 'public interest override' [Section 8(2)]. 'Public interest' is an amorphous concept, which is not defined in access to information legislation. This flexibility is intentional. Legislators and policymakers recognize that the public interest will change over time, according to the circumstances of each situation.

Further, a document may consist of a number of separate 'elements' of information. If certain information within a document is covered by an exemption, a public authority is not absolved from the duty to communicate information contained elsewhere in the document. This may be disclosed by means of 'severability' ('redacted'), that is, documents in which certain exempt items of information have been obscured [Section 10]. The public authorities are obliged to disclose such non-exempt information.

If provision of access would involve an infringement of copyright subsisting in a person other than the state, then that information is exempted under Section 9 and it is an absolute exemption.

Further, certain Intelligence and Security organizations listed in Schedule II of the Act are exempt from the purview of the RTI Act under Section 24. However, even these organizations have to give information relating to allegations of corruption and human rights violations.

## Process for Making a Request for Information and Appeal

The process for acquiring information through RTI is given in the Figure 1.

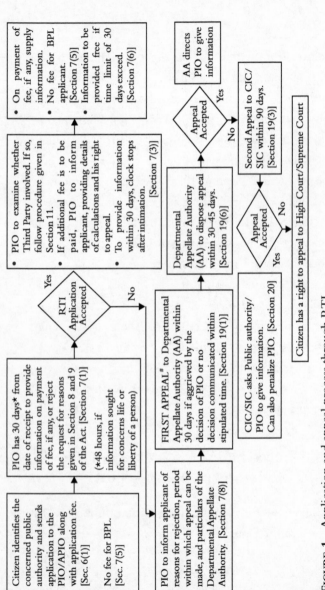

**FIGURE 1** Application and appeal process through RTI

*Note:* # An Applicant can also lodge a complaint with CIC/ SIC for reasons given under Section 18(1) of the Act.

Citizen identifies the concerned public authority and sends application to the PIO/APIO along with application fee. [Sec.6(1)]

No fee for BPL. [Section 7(5)]

PIO has 30 days* from date of receipt to provide information on payment of fee, if any, or reject the request for reasons given in Section 8 and 9 of the Act. [Section 7(1)]

(*48 hours, if information sought for concerns life or liberty of a person)

**RTI Application Accepted**

Yes

- PIO to examine whether Third Party involved. If so, follow procedure given in Section 11.
- If additional fee is to be paid, PIO to inform applicant, providing details of calculations and his right to appeal.
- To provide information within 30 days, clock stops after intimation.

[Section 7(3)]

- On payment of fee, if any, supply information. No fee for BPL applicant. [Section 7(5)]
- Information to be provided free if time limit of 30 days exceed. [Section 7(6)]

No

PIO to inform applicant of reasons for rejection, period within which appeal can be made, and particulars of the Departmental Appellate Authority. [Section 7(8)]

FIRST APPEAL# to Departmental Appellate Authority (AA) within 30 days if aggrieved by the decision of PIO or no decision communicated within stipulated time. [Section 19(1)]

Departmental Appellate Authority (AA) to dispose appeal within 30–45 days. [Section 19(6)]

**Appeal Accepted**

Yes

AA directs PIO to give information

No

Second Appeal to CIC/ SIC within 90 days. [Section 19(3)]

**Appeal Accepted**

Yes

CIC/SIC asks Public authority/ PIO to give information. Can also penalize PIO. [Section 20]

No

Citizen has a right to appeal to High Court/Supreme Court

# 5

# Duties of Information Suppliers

Citizens have a right to information under the Right to Information Act (RTI) Act, from public authorities, which are repositories of information, and this is done through the Public Information Officer (PIO).

## What does 'Public Authority' Mean under the Act?

'Public authority' has been defined in Section 2(h) and it consists of two parts. The first part states that public authority means any authority or body or institution of self-government established or constituted by or under the Constitution, by an enactment made by the Parliament or the State Legislature. It could also be formed by a notification issued or an order by the appropriate Government. The second part starts from the word 'includes' and states that the term 'public authority' includes bodies which are owned, controlled, or substantially financed, directly or indirectly, by funds provided by the appropriate Government, and non-government organizations substantially financed, directly or indirectly, by funds provided by the appropriate Government. If a body satisfies the requirement of the second part, then conditions of the first part need not be satisfied to determine whether it is a 'public authority'.

The terms 'authority', 'body', and 'institution of self-government' have been exhaustively dealt with in *National Stock Exchange of India v. Central Information Commission and Others.*

## Authority

In *Ajay Hasia and Others v. Khalid Mujib Sehravardi and Others,* the Supreme Court quoted with approval the test laid down in *Ramana Dayaram Shetty v. The International Airport Authority of India & Others* for considering a corporation as an authority and therefore 'state' within the meaning of the expression in Article 12. We may summarize the relevant tests gathered from the decision in the *International Airport* case to consider an organization/body as an authority:

1. If the entire share capital of the Corporation is held by the Government.

2. If the financial assistance of the state is so much as to meet almost entire expenditure of the Corporation.

3. It may also be a relevant factor if the Corporation enjoys monopoly status, which is conferred by the state or protected by the state.

4. Existence of deep and pervasive state control may afford the indication that the corporation is a state agency or instrumentality.

5. If the functions of the Corporation are of public importance and closely related to Governmental functions, it would be a relevant factor in classifying the corporation as an instrumentality or agency of the Government.

6. If a department of Government is transferred to a corporation, it would be a strong factor supportive of the thesis that the Corporation is an instrumentality or agency of Government.

If on consideration of these relevant factors it is found that the corporation is an instrumentality or agency of Government, it would be an 'authority', and therefore 'state', within the meaning of the expression in Article 12.

In *Pradeep Kumar Biswas v. Indian Institute of Chemical Biology*, the majority judgment approved of the tests specified in the case of *Ajay Hasia*, and observed as under:

> 40. The picture that ultimately emerges is that the tests formulated in *Ajay Hasia* are not rigid set of principles so that if a body falls within any of them it must, ex hypothesi, be considered to be a State within the meaning of Article 12. The question in each case would be—whether in the light of cumulative facts as established, the body is financially, functionally and administratively dominated by or under the control of the Government. Such control must be particular to the body in question and must be pervasive. If this is found then the body is a State within Article 12. On the other hand, when the control is merely regulatory whether under statute or otherwise, it would not serve to make the body a State.

## *Institution of Self-government*

Institution means an organization or establishment instituted for some specific purpose. In Section 2(h), the word 'institution' is qualified by the words 'self-government'. 'Self-government' refers to the nature of activities that are performed. The activities should be in nature of governmental or public functions, but the institution may be independent and free from governmental control.

'Self-government' will cover and encompass independent, autonomous, self-managed or governed organizations which have been permitted, allowed, and are performing what are regarded as governmental or public functions. Pervasive and deep control of the government is not necessary. An institution which performs public functions and has been created for discharging public or statutory duties as distinguished from private functions can be an 'institution of self-government'.

## *Body*

Second part of Section 2(h) of the Act, specifically deals with 'body'. It consists of two parts. Clause (i) states that a 'body' is owned, controlled, or substantially financed, directly or indirectly, by government. Bodies owned or controlled by government will normally qualify to be 'authorities'. Requirements of conditions laid down in Section 2(h)—(a) to (d)—need not be satisfied and are not required to be examined. Clause (ii) has been interpreted to include private non-government organizations that are substantially financed, directly or indirectly, from government funds. If a body satisfies requirements of clause (i) or (ii), then conditions laid down in Section 2(h)—(a) to (d)—need not be satisfied for qualifying as 'public authority'.

## *Recommendation of Administrative Reforms Commission for NGOs*

The Second Administrative Reforms Commission (ARC) has recommended that organizations which perform functions of a public nature that are ordinarily performed by government or its agencies, and those which enjoy natural monopoly, may be brought within the purview of the RTI Act.

## *Position regarding Public–Private Partnerships (PPPs)*

The Central Information Commission (CIC), in a fully attended meeting on 28 December 2010, suggested that the private companies undertaking government projects should be brought under the RTI Act. Earlier, Information Commissioner Shailesh Gandhi had held that the Delhi International Airport (DIAL), a PPP in which Airport Authority of India has a 26 per cent stake, is a 'public authority', but DIAL got a stay from the Court in May 2011.

The CIC has also written to the Planning Commission to incorporate disclosure norms, so that any project which has the participation of private companies undertaking government projects should be brought under the RTI Act. The Minister of State for Personnel, Public Grievances, and Pensions stated, in the Lok Sabha on 30 November 2011, that any information about PPP which can be disclosed under the RTI Act may be accessed through the public authority which has entered into the said agreement.

## Some Decisions regarding Public Authority

It has been held that any company wholly owned by a public authority, Stock Exchanges, the Supreme Court of India, DISCOMs, National Cooperative Consumers Federation of India Ltd. (NCCF), and National Agriculture Cooperative Marketing Federation of India Ltd. (NAFED) are public authorities. These are evident in cases: *V.T. Gokhale v. UTI Asset Management Company Private Ltd*; *Raj Kumari Agrawal and Others v. Jaipur Stock Exchange Ltd. and National Stock Exchange*; *Subhash Chandra Agrawal v. Supreme Court of India*, *Sarbajit Roy v. Delhi Electricity Regulatory Commission (DERC)*; and *Raj Mangal Prasad, B.M. Verma v. NCCF and NAFED*, respectively.

Punjab and Haryana High Court has held that a crucial touchstone for determining whether an organization qualifies to be a public authority is whether it performs a public duty (see, for instance, *DAV College Trust and Management Society and Others v. Director of Public Institution and Others*).

The Indian Olympic Association (IOA), a society registered under the Societies Registration Act, was also held to be a public authority in *V. Malik v. Indian*

*Olympics Association*. The CIC held that IOA is substantially financed, either directly or indirectly, by the
funds provided by the government, and as such it is
a public authority governed by the provisions of the
RTI Act. The Indian Olympics Association appealed
against this decision in the Delhi High Court. While
confirming that the IOA is a 'public authority', Justice
S. Ravindran (*Indian Olympics Association v. V. Malik
and Others*) held:

> This court therefore concludes that what amounts to
> 'substantial' financing cannot be straight-jacketed into
> rigid formulae, of universal application. Out of neces-
> sity, each case would have to be examined on its own
> facts. That the percentage of funding is not 'majority'
> financing, or that the body is an impermanent one, are
> not material. Equally, that the institution or organiza-
> tion is not controlled, and is autonomous is irrelevant;
> indeed, the concept of non-government organiza-
> tion means that it is independent of any manner of
> government control in its establishment, or manage-
> ment. That the organization does not perform or
> predominantly perform 'public' duties too may not be
> material, as long as the object for funding is achieving
> a felt need of a section of the public, or to secure larger

societal goals. To the extent of such funding, indeed, the organization may be a tool, or vehicle for the executive government's policy fulfilment plan. (para 60)

Recently, the CIC held Delhi Public School, Rohini as a public authority as first, nominees of Delhi Administration (Directorate of Education) hold positions in the Management Committee of the school and second, Delhi Development Authority (DDA), while granting land to the school at a nominal rent/concession rate had laid down that 'DDA reserves the right to alter any terms and conditions on its discretion', thereby establishing its control over the school's use of land. The School had challenged the decision in the High Court of Delhi, and obtained the stay on the order on 23 September 2011 (*The Times of India* 2011).

## Obligations of Public Authorities under the Act

### Key Sections of the Act Enumerating Duties of Public Authorities

• Maintain all its records, duly catalogued and indexed, in a manner and form which facilitates the right to information, and computerize within reasonable time.

Section 4(1)(a)

- Publish within 120 days from the enactment of this Act, 16 types of information, and thereafter update these publications every year.

Section 4(1)(b)

- Publish all relevant facts while formulating important policies which affect the public.

Section 4(1)(c)

- Provide reasons for its administrative or quasi-judicial decisions to affected persons.

Section 4(1)(d)

- To provide as much information, *suo motu*, to the public, through various means.

Section 4(2)

- To disseminate information widely, taking into consideration the cost effectiveness, local language, and so on.

Section 4(3) and Section 4(4)

- Within 100 days of enactment, designate PIOs in all administrative units/offices, as may be necessary.

Section 5(1)

- To designate Assistant Public Information Officer (APIO) within 100 days of enactment at the divisional level/sub-district level, to receive the applications.

  Section 5(2)

- To transfer misdirected requests within five days from the receipt of application, if information is held by another public authority or the subject matter is more closely connected with the functions of another public authority, and inform the applicant immediately about such transfer.

  Section 6(3)

Further, responsibilities of public authority as ordained by CIC/SIC are:

- CIC/SIC has the power to command a public authority to take any such steps as may be necessary to secure compliance with the provision of this Act, including:

  (i) By providing access to information, if so requested, in a particular form;

  (ii) By appointing a Central Public Information Officer (CPIO) or State Public Information Officer, as the case may be;

(iii) by publishing certain information or categories of information;

(iv) by making necessary changes to its practices in relation to the maintenance, management, and destruction of records;

(v) by enhancing the provision of training about the right to information for its officials;

(vi) by providing it with an annual report in compliance with clause (b) of sub-section (1) of Section 4;

Section 19(8)(a)

• To compensate the complainant for any loss or other detriment suffered.

Section 19(8)(b)

## Maintenance of Records

The key obligations of public authorities are given in Section 4 of the Act. It underlines that right to information cannot be fully and effectively implemented without competent records management. Such rights are of little use if reliable records are not created in the first place, or if they cannot be found when needed. Section 4(1)(a) of the Act necessitate maintenance of records duly catalogued and indexed which facilitate right to information. It also states that appropriate records should be computerized and connected through a network.

## *Suo Motu Disclosure of Information*

Section 4(1)(b) requires that every public authority should publish the following 16 categories of information within 120 days of the enactment of the Act (the RTI Act 2005 was enacted on 15 June 2005):

(i) The particulars of its organization, functions, and duties;

(ii) The powers and duties of its officers and employees;

(iii) The procedure followed in the decision-making process, including channels of supervision and accountability;

(iv) The norms set by it for the discharge of its functions;

(v) The rules, regulations, instructions, handbooks, and records, held by it or under its control or used by its employees for discharging its functions;

(vi)   A statement of the categories of documents that are held by it or under its control;

(vii)  The particulars of any arrangement that exists for consultation with, or representation by, the members of the public in relation to the formulation of its policy or implementation thereof;

(viii) A statement of the boards, councils, committees, and other bodies consisting of two or more persons constituted as its part or for the purpose of its advice, and as to whether meetings of those boards, councils, committees, and other bodies are open to the public, or the minutes of such meetings are accessible for public;

(ix)   A directory of its officers and employees;

(x)    The monthly remuneration received by each of its officers and employees, including the system of compensation as provided in its regulations;

(xi)   The budget allocated to each of its agency, indicating the particulars of all plans, proposed expenditures, and reports on disbursements made;

(xii)  The manner of execution of subsidy programmes, including the amounts allocated and the details of beneficiaries of such programs;

(xiii) Particulars of recipients of concessions, permits, or authorizations granted by it;

(xiv) Details in respect of the information, available to or held by it, reduced in an electronic form;

(xv) The particulars of facilities available to citizens for obtaining information, including the working hours of a library or reading room, if maintained for public use;

(xvi) The names, designations, and other particulars of the PIOs;

(xvii) Such other information as may be prescribed; and thereafter update these publications each year.

Publication of this information is not optional. It is a statutory requirement which every public authority is bound to meet. The public authority is also required to update such information every year. It is advisable that as far as possible, the information should be updated as and when any change takes place.

Further, besides the categories of information enumerated earlier, the Government may prescribe other categories of information to be published by any public authority.

The Act further provides that every public authority should provide as much information, *suo motu*, to the public through various means of communications, including internet, so that the public don't need to use the Act to obtain information.

## CENTRAL INFORMATION COMMISSION'S DIRECTIONS ON IMPLEMENTATION OF SECTION 4(1)

The CIC has given detailed direction to public authorities under Section 19(8) of the RTI Act for implementation of Section 4 of the Act. In *Parminder Kaur and Fifty Others*, the Commission directed the Public authorities to, inter-alia, take the following steps:

(i)     The notice board(s) in the offices of all the public authorities should display as much information as practical, about *suo motu* disclosures under Section 4(1)(b) and (c). Further, this information could also be placed in the library or reading room, if such a facility exists, for public convenience.

(ii)    The names, room numbers, telephone numbers, and e-mail addresses of the CPIOs/ACPIOs and Appellate Authorities may be prominently displayed in each office for the convenience of the public at large. If the complete disclosures of 4(1)(b) and (c) are also available with any other officer(s) other than the CPIOs/ACPIOs, the names, designations, room numbers, and telephone numbers of such officers must be prominently displayed in the offices for easy contractibility.

(iii) The public authorities need to ensure that alternate arrangements to accept RTI applications and fee are made when CPIOs proceed on long leave or tours.

(iv) Importantly, no information should be denied merely on the ground that the RTI application has not been submitted in a particular format.

## Duties and Responsibilities of PIOs

Public authorities are the providers of information through their PIOs. The PIO of a public authority plays a pivotal role in making the right of a citizen to information a reality.

The duties of PIOs as given in the RTI Act 2005 are:

- The PIO shall deal with requests from persons seeking information and render reasonable assistance to such persons.

Section 5(3)

- May seek assistance of any other officer for proper discharge of his/her duties.

Section 5(4)

- Render reasonable assistance to person making request orally, to reduce the same in writing.

Section 6(1)

- Disposal of Request within 30 days of receipt of Request, by either providing information about payment of such fee as may be prescribed or reject the request for reasons specified in Sections 8 and 9.

Section 7(1)

- To provide information within 48 hours if information sought concerns life/liberty of a person.

- If information is to be provided on payment of further fee, send intimation to applicant giving details of further fee along with calculations and information concerning his right to review this fee or form of access, providing particulars of Appellate Authority, time limit, and so on.

Section 7(3)

- Assistance to disabled to access records/information.

    Section 7(4)

- If a third party involved, shall take into consideration the representation made by third party under Section 11.

    Section 7(7)

- Where request for information rejected, shall communicate to applicant:
    - Reasons for such rejection
    - Period within which appeal can be preferred.
    - Particulars of the Appellate Authority.

    Section 7(8)

- Information shall ordinarily be provided in the form in which it is sought unless it disproportionately diverts the resources of the public authority or is detrimental to the safety or preservation of the record in question.

    Section 7(9)

The Union Government has issued instructions stating that it has been observed that some people under RTI Act 2005 request the PIO to cull out information from some document(s) and give it in some particular performa devised by them relying on sub-section (9) of

Section 7, which provides that information shall ordinarily be provided in the form in which it is sought. The DoPT clarified that this sub-section simply means that if information is sought in the form of a photocopy, it shall be provided in that form and if it is sought in the form of floppy, it shall be provided in the same form, subject to the conditions given in the Act. It does not mean that the PIO shall reshape the information.

However, Section 7(9) is not meant for denying information. It is more for cases where the applicant has specified a format and the PIO finds it too time consuming to prepare it in that manner. Then he can decide to give it in some other form, the form in which he has the information, or allow for inspection of information and so on. But, if the information is to be culled from quite a number of files/documents or the number of queries is large, recourse to Section 7(9) can be taken by the PIO.

- Where part of information can be provided; PIO shall give notice to Applicant informing about:
  (a) Part of information being provided.
  (b) Reasons for decision.
  (c) Name and designation of the decision-maker.

(d)  Details of fee to be deposited.

(e)  Applicant's right to review the decision regarding non-disclosure, fee, and access.

(f)  Providing Appellate particulars.

Section 10(2)

• If the PIO intends to disclose information supplied by third party and this information has been treated as confidential by the third party:

Within five days of receipt of request, a notice to the third party to make the required submission.

Section 11(1)

• Within 40 days after receipt of request if third party should be given the opportunity to represent and arrive at the decision to disclose or not disclose the information.

Section 11(3)

## Assistance Available to PIO

Under the RTI Act, the PIO is responsible for providing timely information. In case of delays, he or she is subject to penalties. At the same time, it is unlikely that the PIO has all the information sought. The Act recognizes the need to take the assistance of any other officer for the proper discharge of the PIO's duties. The Act makes it clear that the officer whose assistance has been sought shall provide it. For the purpose of any contravention of the provision of this Act, this other officer will be treated as deemed PIO. The relevant provisions in this regard are Sections 5(4) and 5(5).

## Procedure for Transfer of Application

Relevant provision regarding transfer of application is given in Section 6(3) of the Act.

- Once the application is accompanied by the prescribed fee or the below poverty line (BPL) certificate, the PIO should check whether the subject matter of the application or a part of it concerns some other public authority.
- If the subject matter of the application concerns another public authority, it should be transferred to the same. If only a part of the application concerns another public authority, a copy of the application may be sent to the same, clearly specifying the part which relates to it. While transferring the application or sending a copy of it, the concerned public

authority should be informed that the application fee has been received.

- The applicant should also be informed about the transfer of his or her application and the particulars of the public authority to whom the application or a copy of it has been sent.

- Transfer of an application or a part of it, as the case may be, should be made as soon as possible and in any case within five days from the date of receipt of the application. If a PIO transfers an application after five days from the receipt of the application, he or she would be responsible for delay in disposing of the application to the extent of number of days beyond th stipulated five days.

- The PIO of the public authority, to whom the application is transferred, should not refuse acceptance of transfer of the application on the ground that it was not transferred to him or her within five days.

The DoPT issued guidelines as to how to deal with RTI applications received by a public authority regarding information concerning other public authority/authorities. It states that if a person makes an application to a public authority for information, a part of which is available with that public authority and the rest of information is scattered with more than one other public authorities, the PIO of the public authority receiving the application should provide information relating to it and advise the applicant to make separate applications to the concerned public authorities for obtaining information from them. If no part of the information sought is available with it but is scattered with more than one other public authorities, the PIO should inform the applicant that the information is not available with it and that the applicant should make separate applications to the concerned public authorities. It further stated that as the information is not related to any one particular public authority, it is not the case where application should be transferred under sub-section (3) of Section 6 of the Act, which refers to 'another public authority', and not 'other public authorities'.

However, the CIC struck down this guideline of the DoPT in *Chetan Kothari v. Cabinet Secretariat*. The Appellant sought to know petrol expenses incurred by Ministers in Union Government. The Cabinet Secretariat stated that information is not maintained centrally and is scattered across different public authorities. Citing the DoPT instruction, it asked the applicant to file separate RTI applications with different departments to get the information. The Commission stated that the point to be determined is whether Section 6(3) means that the transfer should only be made to one public authority or to multiple public authorities, if required. It noted that Section 13 of the General Clauses Act 1897 stipulates, *inter alia*, that in all central legislations and regulations, unless there is anything repugnant in the subject or context, words in the singular shall include the plural, and vice versa. The Commission stated that there is nothing in the Act which would show that the Parliament intended that the transfer should only be to one public authority. It also appears that DoPT's office memorandum is in contravention of the General Clauses Act 1897 and interpreted Section 6(3) of the Act wrongly. There are numerous instances where RTI applications have been transferred by one public authority to another and none of them appears to know where the information is. In this scenario, for public authorities to take a position that they will transfer to one public authority is unreasonable and the law certainly does not state this.

In view of this, the Commission ruled that DoPT's office memorandum is not consistent with the law and directed the PIO to transfer the RTI application to various public authorities.

## Procedure to be Followed by PIO for Disposal of Request for Information

The procedure for disposal of a request by the PIO is given in Figure 2.

## Fee for Seeking Information

In *Subodh Jain v. Deputy Commissioner of Police, New Delhi and Institute of Company Secretaries of India*, the full bench of the CIC held that,

> ... there is provision for charging of fee, only under Section 6(1) which is the application fee; Section 7(1) which is the fee charged for photocopying etc. and Section 7(5) which is for getting information in printed or electronic format. But there is no provision for any further fee and if any further fee is being charged by the Public Authorities in addition to what is already prescribed under Sections 6(1), 7(1) and 7(5)

133

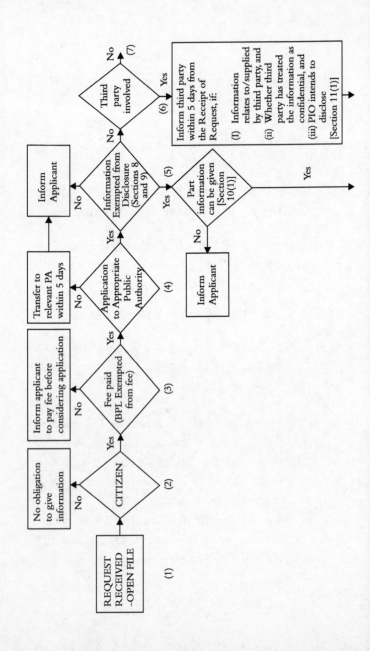

(1) REQUEST RECEIVED –OPEN FILE

(2) CITIZEN
- No → No obligation to give information
- Yes →

(3) Fee paid (BPL Exempted from fee)
- No → Inform applicant to pay fee before considering application
- Yes →

(4) Application to Appropriate Public Authority
- No → Transfer to relevant PA within 5 days
- Yes →

(5) Information Exempted from Disclosure (Sections 8 and 9)
- No → Inform Applicant
- Yes →

Part information can be given [Section 10(1)]
- No → Inform Applicant
- Yes →

(6) Third party involved
- No → (7)
- Yes →

Inform third party within 5 days from the Receipt of Request, if:
(i) Information relates to/supplied by third party, and
(ii) Whether third party has treated the information as confidential, and
(iii) PIO intends to disclose
[Section 11(1)]

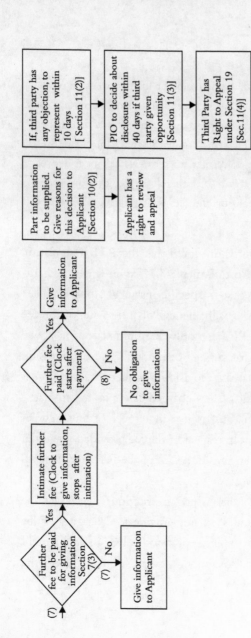

FIGURE 2 Procedure for disposal of request by PIO

of the Act, the same would be in contravention of the RTI Act. The 'further fee' mentioned in Section 7(3) only refers to the procedure in availing of the further fee already prescribed under Section 7(5) of the RTI Act, which is 'further' in terms of the basic fee of Rs 10/-. Section 7(3), therefore, provides for procedure for realizing the fee as prescribed. (Para 40 of the decision)

The Commission noted that the RTI (Regulation of Fee and Cost) Rules 2005 has prescribed charging of actual cost in specific instances along with fee u/s 7(1). The reasonableness, or otherwise, of the fee charged by a PIO can only be in respect of the 'actual cost or price for samples or models'. The Commission concluded that the provision to review the decision as to the amount of fees charged as contained in clause (b) of Section 7(3) is not in respect of any new or further fee but in respect of the fee provided for under Section 7(1) and Section 7(5) of the RTI Act (Para 43 of the decision).

The DoPT has issued instructions that since the Act or the Rules do not provide for charging of fee towards postal expenses or cost involved in deployment of manpower for supply of information and so on, the

PIO should not ask for fee on such account. However, wherever supply of information in a particular form would disproportionately divert the resources of the public authority or would be detrimental to the safety or preservation of the records, the PIO may refuse to supply the information in that form.

Additional fee prescribed by the Regulation of Fee and Cost Rules of the RTI Act 2005 for supply of information is as follows:

(a) Rupees two (Rs 2) for each page (in A4 or A3 size paper) created or copied;

(b) Actual charge or cost price of a copy in larger size paper;

(c) Actual cost or price for samples or models;

(d) For inspection of records, no fee for the first hour; and a fee of rupees five (Rs 5) for each subsequent hour (or a fraction of it);

(e) For information provided in diskette or floppy rupees fifty (Rs 50) per diskette or floppy; and

(f) For information provided in printed form at the price fixed for such publication or rupees two per page of photocopy for extracts from the publication.

# Time Limit for Supply of Information

Table 1 summarizes the time limit for disposal of applications in different situations:

**TABLE 1**   Time Limit for Disposal of Applications

| Sl No. | Situation applications | Time limit for disposing |
|---|---|---|
| 1. | Supply of information in normal course. | Within 30 days of receipt of the request.<br>Section 7(1) |
| 2. | Supply of information if it concerns the life or liberty of a person. | Within 48 hours of receipt of the request.<br>Section 7(1) |
| 3. | Supply of information if the application is received through APIO. | 5 days shall be added to the time period indicated at Sr. Nos 1 and 2.<br>Section 5(2) |
| 4. | Supply of information if application/request is received after transfer from another public authority: | |
| | (a) In the normal course | (a) Within 30 days of the receipt of the application by the concerned public authority.<br>Section 7(1) |
| | (b) In case the information concerns the life or liberty of a person. | (b) Within 48 hours of receipt of the application by the concerned public authority.<br>Section 7(1) |

| | | |
|---|---|---|
| 5. | Supply of information where the applicant is asked to pay an additional fee. | The period between informing the applicant about additional fee and the payment of said fee by the applicant shall be excluded for calculating the period of reply.<br>Section 7(3)(a) |
| 6. | Supply of information by organizations specified in the Second Schedule: | |
| | (a) If information relates to allegations of violation of human rights. | (a) 45 days from the receipt of application<br>Section 24(1) and (4) |
| | (b) In case information relates to allegations of corruption. | (b) Within 30 days of the receipt of application.<br>Section 24(1) |

If the PIO fails to deliver a decision on the request for information within the prescribed period, then he or she shall be deemed to have refused the request [Section 7(2)].

Further, where the specified time limit under Section 7(1) has been transgressed, the CIC issues a showcause notice to the PIO, as to why a penalty of Rs 250 per day, subject to a maximum of Rs 25,000 [under Section 20(1)], should not be imposed on him or her.

# Third Party Information

The Government, in a number of cases, makes inter-departmental consultations. In the process, a public authority may send some confidential papers to another public authority. Can the recipient public authority disclose such confidential papers under the RTI Act? Section 11 of the Act provides the procedure of disclosure of 'third party' information. Third party in relation to the RTI Act means a person other than the citizen who has made request for information. Any public authority other than the one to whom the request has been made shall also be included in the definition of third party [Section (2n)]. If a PIO intends to disclose information supplied by a third party, which the third party has treated as confidential, the PIO, before arriving at a decision to disclose the information shall invite the third party to make a submission in the matter. The third party has a right to make an appeal to the departmental appellate authority (AA) against the decision of the PIO and if not satisfied with the decision of the departmental AA, a second appeal to the Information Commission. The PIO cannot disclose such information unless the procedure prescribed in Section 11 is completed. It is a statuary requirement, non-compliance of which may make the PIO liable to action.

In *Bombay Stock Exchange v. Security and Exchange Board of India*, the full bench of the CIC held that the CPIOs are mandated to send a copy of their orders to the third party, under Section 11(3), from whom objections are sought under Section 11(1). Further, it is not practical to lay down an inflexible rule that PIOs and AAs will always offer an opportunity of hearing to the parties, let alone to the third party. They may do so as per their discretion, keeping in view the complexity of legal and factual issues involved, without forgetting that timelines are to be adhered to, being the essence of the Act. Further, the RTI Act 2005 does not give a third party an automatic veto on disclosure of information pertaining to him, which may be held by a public authority. In *K.K. Mahajan v. Office of Cantonment Board, Dagshai, Himachal Pradesh*, the CIC held that a mere objection by a third party is not enough reason to embargo the disclosure of such information. The law requires application of the CPIO and the appellate authority's minds regarding the pros and the cons of a proposed disclosure, on the basis of the facts of each case, in terms of the norms set out in the Act.

### *Time Limit and Procedure to be Followed when Third Party Information is Involved*

The time limit for the supply of information and the procedures to be followed when a third party is involved are given in Table 2 and Figure 3.

## Imposition of Penalty and Disciplinary Action against PIO

Section 20(1) of the Act provides that the Commission, while deciding a complaint or appeal, shall impose penalties on erring PIOs.

The scale of the penalty to be imposed is Rs 250 for each day of delay, subject to the total amount of such penalty not exceeding Rs 25,000.

Under Section 20(2) of the Act, the Commission can recommend for disciplinary action against the PIO, where the PIO has persistently violated the provisions of the Act.

**TABLE 2**  Time Period for Supply of Information when Third Party is Involved

| Sl No. | Steps involved | Time limit |
|---|---|---|
| 1. | PIO to give written notice of the request for information to the third party that (s)he intends to disclose information to. | Within five days from receipt of the request. Section 11(1) |
| 2. | Third party given opportunity to make representation against the proposed disclosure. | Within 10 days from the date of receipt of the notice from PIO. Section 11(2) |
| 3. | PIO to make decision as to whether or not to disclose the information or record or a part of it and give in writing the notice of his/her decision to the third party. | Within 40 days of receipt of request for obtaining information. Section 11(3) |
| 4. | Third party entitled to appeal against the decision of the PIO. | Within 30 days from the date of order of PIO. Section 19(2) |
| 5. | Appellate Authority to decide on the Appeal. | Within 30 days of receipt of the appeal or within 45 days for reasons to be recorded in writing. Section 19(6) |
| 6. | Second Appeal against the decision of the Appellate Authority lies with the Information Commission. | Within 90 days from the date on which the decision should have been made by Appellate Authority or was actually received. Section 19(3) |

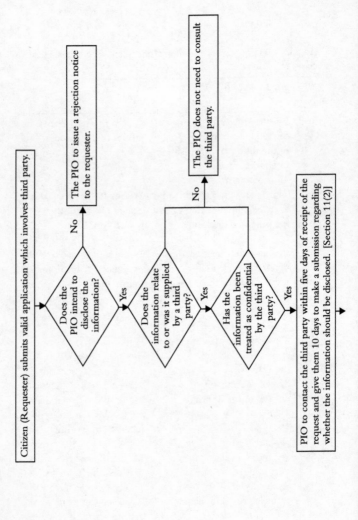

Citizen (Requester) submits valid application which involves third party.

Does the PIO intend to disclose the information?

No → The PIO to issue a rejection notice to the requester.

Yes

Does the information relate to or was it supplied by a third party?

No → The PIO does not need to consult the third party.

Yes

Has the information been treated as confidential by the third party?

No → The PIO does not need to consult the third party.

Yes

PIO to contact the third party within five days of receipt of the request and give them 10 days to make a submission regarding whether the information should be disclosed. [Section 11(2)]

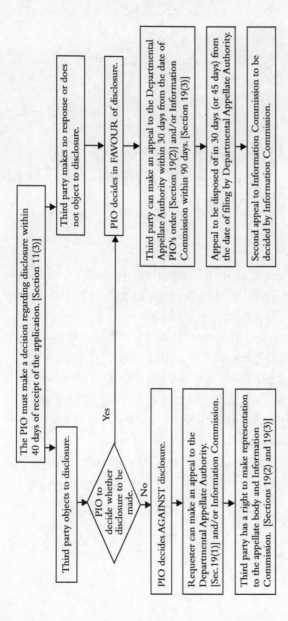

The PIO must make a decision regarding disclosure within 40 days of receipt of the application. [Section 11(3)]

Third party objects to disclosure.

Third party makes no response or does not object to disclosure.

PIO to decide whether disclosure to be made.

Yes

PIO decides in FAVOUR of disclosure.

Third party can make an appeal to the Departmental Appellate Authority within 30 days from the date of PIO's order [Section 19(2)] and/or Information Commission within 90 days. [Section 19(3)]

No

PIO decides AGAINST disclosure.

Requester can make an appeal to the Departmental Appellate Authority. [Sec.19(1)] and/or Information Commission.

Third party has a right to make representation to the appellate body and Information Commission. [Sections 19(2) and 19(3)]

Appeal to be disposed of in 30 days (or 45 days) from the date of filing by Departmental Appellate Authority.

Second appeal to Information Commission to be decided by Information Commission.

**FIGURE 3**  Involvement of a third party

# 6

# Information Exempted from Disclosure

In common with all Freedom of Information Legislations, the Right to Information (RTI) Act 2005 does not provide for a citizen's access to all forms of information. Section 8(1) of the RTI Act provides a list of 10 categories of information, 8(1)(a) to 8(1)(j), as exempted from disclosure. However, under Section 8(2), all such exemptions can be waived if a public authority decides that public interest in disclosure outweighs the harm to protected interests.

Another ground for rejection is under Section 9, where access to information would involve an infringement of copyright subsisting in a person other than the state.

Further, the Act provides in Section 24, that it will not apply to the intelligence and security organizations as specified in the Second Schedule. This at present includes 25 organizations listed under it. However, information pertaining to the allegations of corruption and human rights violations with respect to organizations listed in the Second Schedule is yet to be provided. But information regarding the violation of human rights can be provided only with the approval of the Central or State Information Commission as the case may be.

We will examine each of the exemptions from disclosure in the light of case law.

## Section 8(1): Exemptions from Disclosure of Information

*Notwithstanding anything contained in this Act, there shall be no obligation to give any citizen:*

(a) information, disclosure of which would prejudicially affect the sovereignty and integrity of India, the security, strategic, scientific or economic interests of the State, relation with foreign State or lead to incitement of an offence;

(b) information which has been expressly forbidden to be published by any court of law or tribunal or the disclosure of which may constitute contempt of court;

(c) information, the disclosure of which would cause a breach of privilege of Parliament or the State Legislature;

(d) information including commercial confidence, trade secrets or intellectual property, the disclosure of which would harm the competitive position of a third party, unless the competent authority is satisfied that larger public interest warrants the disclosure of such information;

(e) information available to a person in his fiduciary relationship, unless the competent authority is satisfied that the larger public interest warrants the disclosure of such information;

(f) information received in confidence from foreign Government;

(g) information, the disclosure of which would endanger the life or physical safety of any person or identify the source of information or assistance given in confidence for law enforcement or security purposes;

(h) information which would impede the process of investigation or apprehension or prosecution of offenders;

(i) cabinet papers including records of deliberations of the Council of Ministers, Secretaries and other officers;

Provided that the decisions of Council of Ministers, the reasons thereof, and the material on the basis of which the decisions were taken shall be made public after the decision has been taken, and the matter is complete, or over;

Provided further that those matters which come under the exemptions specified in this section shall not be disclosed;

(j) information which relates to personal information the disclosure of which has no relationship to any public activity or interest, or which would cause unwarranted invasion of the privacy of the individual unless the Central Public Information Officer or the State Public Information Officer or the appellate authority, as the case may be, is satisfied that the larger public interest justifies the disclosure of such information;

Provided that the information which cannot be denied to the Parliament or a State Legislature shall not be denied to any person.

It is for consideration that whether the last proviso is a general one applicable to all the subsections listed under Section 8(1) or only Section 8(1)(j). The division bench of the Bombay High Court in *Surupsingh Hriya Naik v. State of Maharashtra* has held that the proviso has been placed after Section 8(1)(j) and thus applies only to 8(1)(j) and not to other subsections. However, it is opined that the proviso is a general one applicable to all the subsections and limiting it to only 8(1)(j) defeats the very purpose of the RTI Act.

Further in this context, it is stated that Members of Parliament seek information through questions. It is, therefore, important to know the rules of admissibility of these questions. Relevant extracts from the Rules of Procedure and Conduct of Business in Lok Sabha are given in the following sections:

Admissibility of questions

41.(1)  Subject to the provisions of sub-rule (2), a question may be asked for the purpose of obtaining information on a matter of public importance within the special cognizance of the Minister to whom it is addressed.

(2)  The right to ask a question is governed by the following conditions, namely:

(v)  it shall not ask for an expression of opinion or the solution of an abstract legal question or of a hypothetical proposition;

(vi)  it shall not ask as to the character or conduct of any person except in his official or public capacity;

(viii)  it shall not relate to a matter which is not primarily the concern of the Government of India;

(ix)  it shall not ask about proceedings in the Committee which have not been placed before the House by a report from the Committee;

(x)  it shall not reflect on the character or conduct of any person whose conduct can only be challenged on a substantive motion;

(xi) it shall not make or imply a charge of a personal character;

(xii) it shall not raise questions of policy too large to be dealt with within the limits of an answer to a question;

(xiii) it shall not repeat in substance questions already answered or to which an answer has been refused;

(xiv) it shall not ask for information on trivial matters;

(xv) it shall not ordinarily ask for information on matters of past history;

(xvi) it shall not ask for information set forth in accessible documents or in ordinary works of reference;

(xvii) it shall not raise matters under the control of bodies or persons not primarily responsible to the Government of India;

(xviii) it shall not ask for information on matter which is under adjudication by a court of law having jurisdiction in any part of India;

(xix)    it shall not relate to a matter with which a Minister is not officially concerned;

(xx)     it shall not refer discourteously to a friendly foreign country;

(xxi)    it shall not seek information about matters which are in their nature secret, such as composition of Cabinet Committees, Cabinet discussions, or advice given to the President in relation to any matter in respect of which there is a constitutional, statutory or conventional obligation not to disclose information;

(xxii)   it shall not ordinarily ask for information on matters which are under consideration of a Parliamentary Committee; and

(xxiii)  it shall not ordinarily ask about matters pending before any statutory tribunal or statutory authority performing any judicial or quasijudicial functions or any commission or court of enquiry appointed to enquire into, or investigate, any matter but may refer to

matters concerned with procedure or
subject or stage of enquiry, if it is not
likely to prejudice the consideration of
the matter by the tribunal or commission or court of enquiry.

Questions on matters of correspondence between
Government of India and State Governments

42.     In matters which are or have been the subject
of correspondence between the Government
of India and the Government of a State, no
questions shall be asked except as to matters
of fact, and the answer shall be confined to a
statement of fact.

## *Exemption 1: Disclosure Affecting Security, Economic Interests, and Relationship with Foreign States*

Section 8(1)(a): *Information, disclosure of which would
prejudicially affect the sovereignty and integrity of India, the
security, strategic, scientific or economic interests of the State,
relation with foreign State or lead to incitement of offence.*

For an example of 'economic' interest of the state,
we may refer to *Kamal Anand v. Central Board of Direct
Taxes*. The appellant sought departmental guidelines

relating to the scrutiny policy for non-corporate assessee during the financial year 2006–7. The Central Public Information Officer (CPIO) denied this under Section 8(1)(a), because it would prejudicially affect the economic interests of the state. The first appellate authority (AA), while upholding the decision of CPIO, stated that if detailed guidelines are made public, then any unscrupulous taxpayer could adjust his declaration of income to avoid verification by the income tax officer.

In the second appeal to the Central Information Commission (CIC), the appellant requested for information related to the previous financial year, and since that period is over, it can be disclosed without any policy implication. On behalf of the public authority it was stated that every year a large number of Income Tax returns are filed by taxpayers. Only a small percentage of them are taken up for scrutiny. The Income Tax Department issues guidelines for selection of cases for scrutiny for the use of the assessing officers of the department. If the guidelines for selection of cases are made public, these are liable to be misused by some unscrupulous taxpayers to evade taxes at will. Further, the department was of the view that the disclosure of scrutiny guidelines would not serve any public interest and will, on the contrary, adversely affect the economic interests of the state, by facilitating offence of tax evasion. It was also submitted that the submissions are being submitted after approval of the Union Finance Minister.

The Full Bench of the Commission held that it is certainly within the domain of the concerned public authority to decide and determine whether or not disclosure would adversely affect the economic interest of the state. The Commission, therefore, can only look into as to whether the determination by the department about the probable effect of a particular policy disclosure is based on objective criteria or as to whether the department has arrived at a particular conclusion in a reasoned manner, as opposed to an arbitrary one. The Commission further stated that as the implications of disclosure have been put to the closest scrutiny, it cannot enter into the adequacy of the criteria taken into account by the concerned public authority, and that it cannot surpass an objective consideration and replace it with its own subjective consideration. When a denial is covered by an exemption clause under Section 8 of the RTI Act, so long as such application of exemption is based on objective criteria and is not arrived at in an arbitrary manner, the Commission does not intend to interfere.

For an example of 'security' interest of the state, we may refer to *S.C. Sharma v. Ministry of Home Affairs*. The Commission in this case held that the matters connected with the interception of telephones that were governed by the provisions of Indian Telegraph Act 1885 were distinctly related to the security of India. In that sense, disclosure of the category of information requested by the appellant will attract provisions of Section 8(1)(a) of the RTI Act.

## Exemption 2: Disclosure Forbidden by Courts/Tribunals

Section 8(1)(b): *Information which has been expressly forbidden to be published by any court of law or tribunal or the disclosure of which may constitute contempt of court.*

The only exemption in a sub-judice matter is what has been expressly forbidden from disclosure by a court or a Tribunal and what may constitute contempt of court. *K.M. Talera v. Cantonment Board, Pune* serves as an important example of such an exemption.

There is no exemption from disclosure for sub-judice matters. This is relevant in *Vishwanath Poddar v. Ministry of Company Affairs.*

## Exemption 3: Disclosure Causing Breach of Privilege of Parliament / State Legislature

Section 8(1)(c): *Information, the disclosure of which would cause a breach of privilege of Parliament or the State Legislature.*

This exemption preserves the Parliament's sole power to control its own business, specifically in relation to the disclosure of information. An infringement of Parliamentary privilege would, for example, arise if a public authority reveals the private deliberations of a Parliamentary Select Committee.

In *Priya Pal Bhante v. Rajya Sabha Secretariat*, the Commission held that the proceedings of a Select/ Joint Committee are not disclosable unless placed before the Parliament/Legislature.

In *Manohar Parrikar and Others v. Accountant General, Goa, Orissa, and Punjab*, the full Commission held:

... that while all evidences and depositions before the Parliamentary Committees are no doubt held secret as well as all proceedings before it, it cannot be stretched to mean that every single item of information held anywhere, that may or in near future, become part of the proceeding before the Parliamentary Committee, or may be required to be produced as evidence before it, should also come under the exemption from disclosure. While all evidence or material, which is part of a proceeding before a Committee of Parliament, has to remain secret until the Committee wills otherwise, every other material, which does not answer that description is beyond the bar. In other words, while the actual material in a proceeding before a Parliamentary Committee is prohibited from disclosure, such prohibition would not apply to such material, which is not yet part of an ongoing proceeding. (para 32)

## *Exemption 4: Disclosure Harming Competitive Position of Third Party*

Section 8(1)(d): *Information including commercial confidence, trade secrets or intellectual property, the disclosure of which would harm the competitive position of a third party, unless the competent authority is satisfied that larger public interest warrants the disclosure of such information.*

Information relating to public action regarding purchase processes is under public domain and not exempted.

In *N. Anbarasan v. Indian Overseas Bank, Chennai,* the Commission held that the information sought relate to the public action with regard to the processes that have been followed in the purchase of computers and other accessories. Such actions clearly fall under the public domain and therefore exemption claimed under Section 8(1)(d) is not justified.

### ANY COMMERCIAL AGREEMENT BETWEEN A PUBLIC AUTHORITY AND A THIRD PARTY IS A PUBLIC DOCUMENT AVAILABLE FOR ACCESS TO A CITIZEN UNLESS COVERED UNDER SECTION 8(1)(D)

In *S.K. Maheshwari v. Telecommunications Consultants India Ltd.* (TCIL), the appellant, *inter alia*, sought for documents relating to the agreement executed between Mokhtar Ibrahim Saddi and TCIL. It was denied on the ground that a confidentiality clause existed and, as per Section 11 of the RTI Act (Third Party Information), the second signatory to the agreement had not agreed for disclosure. Therefore, the exemption under Section 8(1)(d) came into application. The Commission held that the decision of the CPIO and the AA with regard to furnishing a copy of the agreement (applying the provisions of Section 11) is not valid as any commercial agreement between a public authority and a third party is a public document. It should hence be accessible to any citizen, except on the grounds of commercial confidentiality, the like would specifically be exempted under Section 8(1)(d).

INFORMATION MAY BE DENIED IF THERE IS A
CONFIDENTIALITY CLAUSE IN THE COLLABORATION
AGREEMENT BETWEEN A PUBLIC AUTHORITY AND
ITS COLLABORATOR PROHIBITING DISCLOSURE TO
A THIRD PARTY

In *Anil Kumar v. ITI, Bangalore*, the appellant sought for certain information in relation to ITI's collaboration with Alcatel. The information was denied invoking Section 8(1)(d) of the RTI Act. Further it was stated that since this information was governed by legal cooperation norms with the company's collaborator, it would prohibit disclosure to a third party.

The Commission noted that so far as OCB283 technology switches are concerned, the collaboration agreement with Alcatel has a confidentiality clause by which ITI has agreed not to disclose any technical knowhow received under the agreement. The information sought by the appellant, if furnished, would be in breach of the said confidentiality clause and, as such, the CIC upheld the declining of information.

## DISCLOSURE OF EVALUATION PROCESS OF TENDERS COMES UNDER THIRD PARTY INFORMATION

The High Court of Delhi in *Bharat Sanchar Nigam Ltd. (BSNL) v. Chander Sekhar,* dealt with the case where the respondent had sought from the appellant the evaluation report of GSM Phase VI tender on the financial bids which were opened. Initially, the CPIO and the first appellant authority had denied the same on the ground that the information sought of was 'commercial confidence' in nature and exempted under Section 8(1)(d). The CIC, however, ruled that as evaluation process stood completed, the commercial position of the bidders could not be adversely affected by such disclosure and as such exemption under Section 8(1)

(d) is not available. This was so as the information was already in public domain owing to finalization and completion of the bidding process. Further, the CIC held that it was in the larger public interest to disclose such information, and the Non-Disclosure Agreements were valid only till the opening of the bids.

The BSNL's contention before the High Court was that since the case pertaining to GSM Phase VI was being examined *qua* the allegation of irregularity, the competent authority has cancelled the tender and, as such, no contract came into existence. Thus, no question of giving any kind of information arose. Besides this, making public the confidential information of the tenderers particularly in view of signing of Non-Disclosure Agreements would certainly affect the goodwill of the appellant. This would affect the number of participating tenderers in subsequent tenders resulting in monetary loss due to reduction in competition.

The respondent argued that the commercial confidentiality of bids is over once financial bids are opened and prices including details are disclosed to all the bidders.

The Court observed that the perusal of Freedom of Information (FOI) Act in US and well as UK reveal that there is an exemption from disclosure of trade secrets and confidential commercial and financial information obtained from a person. The reason being that such disclosure is likely to impair the government's ability to obtain necessary information in future or to cause substantial harm to the competitive position of a person from whom information is obtained. Further, the test regarding confidentiality of information submitted with the bids is whether such information is generally available for public perusal. If this is not so, it is treated as confidential.

The Court observed in this case that the tender process was scrapped and the Non-Disclosure Agreement, which extended the obligation of confidentiality beyond the date of opening of tenders for a period of two years, has also elapsed. It ruled that the disclosure of such information which is part of the evaluation process would still require the third party procedure under Section 11 of the Act. Besides the bid price, there may still be information in the bid which may have been discussed in the evaluation process of commercial confidence containing trade secrets or intellectual property of the bidders.

## *Exemption 5: Information Available in a Fiduciary Relationship*

Section 8(1)(e): *Information available to a person in his fiduciary relationship, unless the competent authority is satisfied that the larger public interest warrants the disclosure of such information.*

The word 'fiduciary' is derived from the Latin *fiducia*, meaning 'trust', a person (including a juristic person such as a government, a university, or a bank) who has the power and obligation to act for another under circumstances which require total trust, good faith, and honesty.

Some important decisions relating to this Section are listed in the following sections.

### ACR IS DISCLOSABLE

The Supreme Court of India in *Dev Dutt v. Union of India and Others* dealt with an appeal preferred by an employee of the Border Roads Engineering Service against the denial of promotion as Superintending Engineer. As per the DPC guidelines for this post the benchmark should be a rating of 'very good' for the last five years. The appellant was not considered for promotion as in one of the last five years, his report was 'good'. However, he was not communicated the 'good' entry. His contention was that had he been communicated that entry, he would have had an opportunity of making a representation for upgrading it. He contended that the rules of natural justice have been violated by such non-communication.

The Apex Court held that non-communication of an entry in the ACR of a public servant is arbitrary because it deprives the employee concerned from making a representation against it and praying for its upgradation. Hence, such non-communication violates Article 14 of the Constitution. The Court further stated that the rules of natural justice are not codified nor are they unvarying in all situations; rather they are flexible. They may, however, be summarized in one word: fairness. Of course, what is fair would depend on the situation and the context. Originally there were said to be only two principles of natural justice, the rule against bias, and the right to be heard (audi alteram patem). However, with time, more rules of natural justice have evolved. Thus natural justice has an expanding content and is not stagnant.

The following (paragraphs 39 to 41 of the judgment) sums up the Court's decision on this matter.

In the present case, we are developing the principles of natural justice by holding that fairness and transparency in public administration requires that all entries (whether poor, fair, average, good or very good) in the Annual Confidential Report of a public servant, whether in civil, judicial, police or any other State service (except the military), must be communicated to him within a reasonable period so that he can make a representation for its upgradation. This in our opinion is the correct legal position even though there may be no Rule/G.O. requiring communication of the entry, or even if there is a Rule/G.O. prohibiting it, because the principle of non-arbitrariness in State action as envisaged by Article 14 of the Constitution in our opinion requires such communication. Article 14 will override all rules or government orders.

We further hold that when the entry is communicated to him the public servant should have a right to make a representation against the entry to the concerned authority, and the concerned authority must decide the representation in a fair manner and within a reasonable period. We also hold that the representation must be decided by an authority higher than the one who gave the entry, otherwise the likelihood is that the representation will be summarily rejected without adequate consideration as it would be an appeal from Caesar to Caesar. All this would be conducive to fairness and transparency in public administration, and would result in fairness to public servants. The State must be a model employer, and must act fairly towards its employees. Only then would good governance be possible.

We, however, make it clear that the above directions will not apply to military officers because the position for them is different as clarified by this Court in *Union of India v. Major Bahadur Singh*, 2006 (1) SCC 368. But they will apply to employees of statutory authorities, public sector corporations and other instrumentalities of the State (in addition to Government servants).

### DOPT INSTRUCTIONS ON THE
### DISCLOSURE OF ACR

Subsequent to the judgment of the Supreme Court in *Dev Dutt v. Union India*, on 12 May 2008, the Government of India, Department of Personnel issued an office memorandum on 14 May 2009, that the Annual Confidential Report will be modified as

Annual Performance Assessment Report (APAR) and the full APAR including the overall grade and assessment of integrity shall be communicated to the concerned officer. The concerned officer shall be given the opportunity to make any representation against the entries and the final grading given in the Report. This new system is applicable prospectively, with effect from the reporting period 2008–9.

### DISCLOSURE OF EVALUATED ANSWER SHEETS, CUT–OFF MARKS, AND QUESTION–WISE MARKS

In *Central Board of Secondary Education and Anr. v. Aditya Bandopadhyay and Others*, the respondent appeared for the Secondary School Examination 2008 conducted by CBSE. Not satisfied with the result, he applied for inspection and re-evaluation of his answer books. This was rejected stating that, (i) information sought is exempted under Section 8(1)(e) of the RTI Act since CBSE shared fiduciary relationship with its evaluators, (ii) examination bye-laws of the board provide no re-evaluation or disclosure or inspection of answer books, and (iii) the CIC in one of its full bench decision had ruled out such disclosure by CBSE.

The respondent filed a writ petition in the Calcutta High Court. The CBSE contended that about 12 to 13 lakh candidates across the country appear in class X and XII examinations which generate as many as 60 to 65 lakh answer books. As per Examination Bye-law No. 62, it maintains answer books only for a period of three months. If re-evaluation or inspection of answer books is permitted, it will create confusion and chaos, subjecting its elaborate system of examinations to delay and disarray. It further submitted that the procedure evolved and adopted by it ensures fairness and accuracy in evaluation of answer books and made the entire process as foolproof as possible.

The Division Bench of the High Court stated that the evaluated answer books of an examinee, being a 'document, manuscript, record, and opinion' fell within the definition of 'information' as defined in Section 2(f) of the RTI Act. It further held that the examining bodies were bound to provide inspection of evaluated answer books to the examinees. The High Court, however, rejected re-evaluation of the answer books, as that was not a relief available under RTI Act. The RTI Act only provided the right to access information, and not for any consequential reliefs.

Feeling aggrieved by this decision, CBSE filed the appeal before the Supreme Court. Justice Raveendran, while delivering the judgment held that an examining body does not hold the evaluated answer books in a fiduciary relationship, qua the examiner. In case the information is not available to an examining body in its fiduciary relationship, the exemption under Section 8(1)(e) is not valid. The Court further held that if the rules and regulations governing the functioning of a public authority require preservation of information for only a limited period, the applicant will be entitled to the same only if he seeks the information when it is available with the public authority. The Apex Court affirmed the order of the Calcutta High Court directing the examining bodies to permit examinees to inspect their answer books.

Prior to this case, the full bench of CIC dealt with disclosure of evaluated answer sheets *Rakesh Kumar Singh and others v. Lok Sabha and others*. The Commission held that in regard to public examinations conducted by institutions established by the Constitution, like the UPSC or institutions established by any enactment by the Parliament or Rules made by it, like CBSE, Staff Selection Commission, Universities, and so on, the function of which is mainly to conduct examinations and which have an established system as foolproof as that can be, and which, by their own rules or regulations prohibit disclosure of evaluated answer sheets or where the disclosure of evaluated answer sheets would result in rendering the system unworkable in practice, a citizen cannot seek disclosure of the evaluated answer sheets under the RTI Act 2005 (para 39). Further, insofar as examinations conducted by other public authorities, the main function of which is not of conducting examinations, the disclosure of the answer sheets shall be the general rule but each case may have to be examined individually to see as to whether disclosure of evaluated answer sheets would render the system unworkable in practice (para 40).

However, later on the CIC took a different stand in *Manoj Kumar Pathak v. CBSE*. The Commission did not agree with the full Bench decision and held that the matter has to be decided on the basis of the RTI Act only. The onus of proving that the denial was justified fell on the PIO and as the PIO was unable to advance reasonable reason for denying the information, he should provide the answer-wise marks to the appellant.

## DPC MINUTES ARE DISCLOSABLE

In *Rakesh Kumar Singh and Others v. Lok Sabha Secretariat and Others*, the full bench of the Commission held that the proceedings of the Departmental Promotion Committees or its Minutes are not covered by any of the exemptions provided for under Section 8(1) and, therefore, such proceedings and minutes are to be disclosed. Disclosure of proceedings of Departmental Promotion Committee (DPC) and Selection Committee meeting was also affirmed by the Commission in *Sharda P. Meshram v. DoPT*, *Jyoti Legha v. UPSC*, and *N.M. Chavda v. UPSC*.

### PROVISION REGARDING QUESTION BOOKLET, ANSWER KEY, AND SO ON, CONSTITUTING PART OF LIMITED QUESTION BANK

In *B.L. Goel v. AIIMS*, the appellant sought a copy of the question paper for the MD/MS entrance examination (containing 300 questions), a copy of the correct answer sheet to all 300 questions, and a copy of the mark sheet with the rank of a candidate who appeared in the examination. AIIMS denied disclosing the question paper and the correct answer sheet as it held that this disclosure would deplete its question bank.

The Commission stated that under normal circumstances, there should not be any objection to hand over the question paper as well as answer keys to the candidates. However, after scrutinizing the AIIMS committee report and the submissions made by the CPIO and AA during the hearing, the Commission concluded that AIIMS is taking all precautions in conducting examinations in the most satisfactory manner, and that they have also evolved a foolproof system comprising several in-built checks. Keeping all such aspects, the CIC upheld the decision of the Institute.

However, this decision was overruled by the Commission in *Mangla Ram Jat v. Banaras Hindu University*. In this case, the appellant sought the complete text of the question paper to the MD/MS Examination 2008 along with the standard answer key. The Commission held that any refusal of information has to be only on one or more grounds mentioned in Section 8(1) or Section 9. The Act gives no scope to the adjudicating authorities to import new exemptions other than those that have been provided under it and, thereby, deny the information. Further, the Commission stated that after 'going through the decision in *B.L. Goel v. AIIMS* relied upon by the respondent, the Commission finds that none of the exemptions as required under the Act to deny information have been relied upon by the Hon'ble Commission while deciding the said appeal'.

## Exemption 6: Information Received in Confidence from Foreign Government

Section 8(1)(f): *Information received in confidence from foreign Government.*

In *Arun Jaitely v. CBI*, the appellant sought information regarding the correspondence exchanged between the Crown Prosecution Service of the United Kingdom, the Interpol, and the CBI, relating to the freezing and de-freezing of the Bank accounts of Ottavio Quattrocchi and other ongoing investigations. The CBI claimed exemption on the ground that communications with other external agencies which are cooperating on the matter are 'privileged communications' and hence exempt from disclosure as under Sections 8(1)(f) and 8(1)(e).

The Commission upheld this decision while observing that the CBI had been investigating the case for nearly 16 years without much success and, such exemptions would not be applicable after the expiry of 20 years. The CBI was, therefore, advised to expedite the investigations.

## Exemption 7: Disclosure Endangering Life/Physical Safety

Section 8(1)(g): *Information, the disclosure of which would endanger the life or physical safety of any person or identify the source of information or assistance given in confidence for law enforcement or security purposes.*

### DISCLOSING DETAILS OF CASE DIARY BY POLICE EXEMPTED

In *Kuldeep Kumar v. Commissioner of Police, New Delhi*, the appellant sought 'date-wise details of each and every investigational step(s) undertaken by the police to examine the suspects and others thoroughly'. The police authorities contended that the information sought forms part of the police case diary—a privileged document. The Commission agreed with the appellate authority's averment that disclosing the details of the case diary will have far-reaching consequences. This applied specifically to the confidentiality of the information received by the police and, may even endanger the physical safety of those cross-examined by the police authorities.

## Exemption 8: Disclosure Impeding the Process of Investigation

Section 8(1)(h): *Information which would impede the process of investigation or apprehension or prosecution of offenders.*

In *Bhagat Singh v. CIC*, the petitioner's wife had filed a criminal complaint against him that she had spent/paid dowry of Rs 10 lakhs. Alleging that these claims were false, the petitioner, in order to defend himself, approached the Income Tax Department with a tax evasion petition (TEP). The petitioner requested the Director of Income Tax (Investigation) for the status of the hearing and TEP proceedings. On failing to obtain response, he filed an RTI application to ascertain the fate of his TEP. The CPIO rejected the application under Section 8(1)(j), that is, personal information which has no relationship with any public activity. The appellate authority also rejected the request for information and beside Section 8(1)(j), also invoked Section 8(1)(h), that is, information which would impede the process of investigation or apprehension or prosecution of offenders.

Against this order, the petitioner filed a second appeal before the CIC. The CIC instructed the Director of Income Tax (Investigation) to disclose the report after the entire process of investigation and tax recovery (if any) is complete.

The petitioner in a writ petition to the High Court of Delhi requested to partially quash the order of CIC in-so-far as it directs the disclosure after the entire process of investigation and tax recovery is complete.

The Court stated that access to information under Section 3 of the RTI Act is the rule and exemptions under Section 8, the exception. Section 8 being a restriction on this fundamental right, must therefore be strictly construed. It should not be interpreted in manner as to shadow the very right itself. Under Section 8, exemption from releasing information is granted if it would impede the process of investigation or the prosecution of the offenders. It is apparent that the mere existence of an investigation process cannot be a ground for refusal of the information; the authority withholding information must show satisfactory reasons as to why the release of such information would hamper the investigation process. Such reasons should be germane, and the inference of the process being hampered should be reasonable and based on some material. Sans this consideration, Section 8(1)(h) and other such provisions would become the haven for dodging demands for information.

Further, a rights based enactment is akin to a welfare measure. The Act, should receive a liberal interpretation. The contextual background and history of the Act is such that the exemptions, outlined in Section 8, relieving the authorities from the obligation to provide information, constitute restrictions on the exercise of the rights provided by it. Therefore, such exemption provisions have to be construed in their terms. This view has been supported in *Nathi Devi v. Radha Devi Gupta*, *B.R. Kapoor v. State of Tamil Nadu*, and *V. Tulasamma v. Sesha Reddy*. Adopting a different approach would result in narrowing the rights and approving a judicially mandated class of restriction on the rights under the Act, which is unwarranted.

The Court further observed that in the present case, the orders of the respondents do not reflect any reasons why the investigation process would be hampered. The petitioner's grouse against the condition imposed by the CIC is all the more valid since he claims it to be of immense relevance, to defend himself in criminal proceedings.

The Court held that as to the issue of whether the investigation has been complete or not, the petitioner seeks access to the preliminary investigation reports pursuant to which notices under Sections 131, 143(2), 148 of the Income Tax have been issued and not as to the outcome of the investigation and reassessment carried on by the Assessing Officer. Therefore, without a disclosure as to how the investigation process would be hampered by sharing the materials collected till the notices were issued to the assesse, the respondents could not have rejected the request for granting information.

### WHEN INVESTIGATION OR PROSECUTION CAN BE CONSIDERED STILL PENDING AND DISCLOSURE OF INFORMATION WOULD IMPEDE THE PROCESS

In *C. Seetharamaiah v. Commissionerate of Customs and Central Excise,* the appellant's son was facing prosecution under the Prevention of Corruption Act in the CBI Court. He asked, under RTI, the correspondence of CBI with the respondent public authority in this regard, which he claimed is necessary to prove the innocence of his son in the ongoing prosecution in the Trial Court. This was denied and the matter came before the Commission. The respondents and the CBI (the Third Party) argued that an accused in an ongoing prosecution should not be allowed to access any information which may be evidence in that prosecution independent of the Trial Court. An accused in an ongoing prosecution is free to demand access to any information for his defence and the Trial Court, after considering the matter—in which the prosecuting side is also given a chance to present its arguments—makes a decision about whether or not to abide by a request made by the accused. This is a matter which is entirely within the jurisdiction and the discretion of the Trial Court. To allow an accused access to a set of information known to be related to an ongoing prosecution through action under the RTI Act would amount to prejudging the matter for the Trial Court and hence would impede the prosecution in progress. The majority decision of the Commission held that they agree with the respondents that the integrity of a criminal proceeding before a Trial Court in matters of what to allow to be produced as evidence should be taken by the Court itself and not otherwise. Under criminal laws, a public authority is authorized not to produce a certain information or record in the Trial Court unless so directed by the Court itself. Forcing the public authority to part with any such information—which it would otherwise not have disclosed before the Trial Court—through an RTI proceeding would amount to imposing on the prosecuting public authority a burden it is not obliged to bear. It is, therefore, important that all determinations about disclosure of any information relating to an ongoing prosecution should be through the Trial Court and not otherwise. However, there was one dissent decision note which stated that the information needed to be disclosed and is not exempt under Section 8(1) (e) or (h).

In *Dugesh Kumari v. Income Tax Department,* a criminal case was instituted against the appellant and she sought copy of the sanction file through an RTI application. This was denied under Section 8(1)(h). Before the Commission, the appellant's contention was that information cannot be denied as she has been convicted and her appeal against conviction is presently pending in the High Court. According to her, the process of prosecution is over and the matter cannot be said to be under prosecution any more in terms of Section 8(1)(h) of the RTI Act. On the other hand, CBI argued that the completion of trial and conviction does not mean that the process of prosecution is over in terms of Section 8(1)(h). That the appeal is pending before the High Court is indicative of the fact that the process of 'prosecution' is still continuing and is not yet over. Reliance was also placed on the Delhi High Court judgment dated 10 November 2006 in WP(C) No. 16712/2006 (*Surinder Pal Singh v. Union of India*) in which it has been held that when a case is under prosecution, disclosure of any information with regard to it may impede the prosecution of the offenders.

The majority decision opined that the process of 'prosecution' is not yet over and is still continuing, for, it is open to the court to affirm, modify, or reverse the trial court judgment. The process of prosecution can be said to be over when all judicial remedies have been fully exhausted. The dissenting decision notice, while agreeing that in view of the pendency of the appeal in the High Court, the matter is under prosecution in terms of Section 8(1)(h), did not agree that disclosure would impede the process of prosecution as contemplated under Section 8(1)(h).

## *Exemption 9: Cabinet Papers*

Section 8(1)(i): *Cabinet papers including records of deliberations of the Council of Ministers, Secretaries and other officers:*

> Provided that the decisions of Council of Ministers, the reasons thereof, and the material on the basis of which the decisions were taken shall be made public after the decision has been taken, and the matter is complete, or over.
>
> Provided further that those matters which come under the exemptions specified in this section shall not be disclosed.

As can be seen Section 8(1)(i) has two provisos. First, a decision of the Council of Ministers and the material on the basis of which that decision is made has to be made public, 'after the decision has been taken and the matter is complete or over.' Second, there shall be no disclosure under the first proviso if the information otherwise attracts exemption provisions of Section 8.

## *Exemption 10: Personal Information*

Section 8(1)(j): *Information which relates to personal information the disclosure of which has no relationship to any public activity or interest, or which would cause unwarranted invasion of the privacy of the individual unless the Central Public Information Officer or the State Public Information Officer or the appellate authority, as the case may be, is satisfied that the larger public interest justifies the disclosure of such information.*

The right to privacy is one of the fundamental rights recognized the world over. David Banisar and Simon Davies of Privacy International have chronicled privacy law in as many as 53 countries in the world (Banisar and Davies 1999).

The Right to Privacy means the right to be left alone and the right of a person to be free from unwarranted publicity. Even though the 'right to privacy', by itself, has not been identified by our constitution, and though as a concept is too broad and moralistic to define judicially, the Supreme Court of India has established by its liberal interpretation that the Right is an integral part of the Right to Personal Liberty under Article 21 of the Constitution (see, for instance, *Kharak Singh v. the State of UP* and *R. Rajagopal v. State of TN*).

It is recognized all over that privacy is not to be violated unless there are good and sufficient reasons to disclose, as the concerned party may suffer incalculable and irretrievable harm by unjustified disclosures. The CIC, in a number of decisions, had not allowed disclosure of income-tax returns, PAN numbers, details filed for tax determination, bank accounts, sources of funds, partnership details, and so on. Information which identifies ailment of an employee/diagnosis of disease is exempted from disclosure. A relevant case would be *H.C. Verma v. Indian Oil Corporation*.

However, there may be situations like HIV-positive patient who may transmit the disease to his or her prospective spouse may not be entitled to maintenance of confidentiality since the life of the spouse is at stake. In *Mr. 'X' v. Hospital*, a two-judge Bench of the Supreme Court of India held that since HIV is fatal and the life of the spouse has to be saved, the right to privacy of the patient is not absolute in this situation. There is nothing wrong if the Hospital informs the prospective spouse of Mr X's HIV status. As such, disclosure to the partner about the HIV status of the spouse was held valid.

The income tax returns, movable and immovable property, details of investment, lending and borrowing, gifts accepted, etc., are 'personal information' which stand exempted from disclosure unless involving larger public interest. The performance of an employee in an organization is primarily a matter between the employee and the employer and normally those aspects and governed by the service rules which fall under the expression 'personal information', the disclosure of which would cause unwarranted invasion of privacy of that individual, unless larger public interest justifies disclosure. As such, details of salary, showcause notices, orders of censure, oblique punishment issues to an employee, etc., qualify to be personal information under Section 8(i)(j). This was decided by the Supreme Court of India on 3 October 2012 in *Girish Ramchandra Deshpande v. CIC and Others*.

When a citizen seeks information concerning himself, the same cannot be denied under Section 8(1)(j). This is evident in *Rakesh Kumar Singh and Others v. Lok Sabha Secretariat & Others*, *Manohar Singh v. NTPC*, and

*Er. Ranjan Das v. Swami Vivekanand National Institute of Rehabilitation Training & Research, Cuttack.*

## Exemption 11: Absolute Exemption—Infringement of Copyright Subsisting in a Person Other than the State (Section 9)

Section 9 reads:

> Without prejudice to the provisions of Section 8, a Central Public Information Officer or a State Public Information Officer, as the case may be, may reject a request for information where such a request for providing access would involve an infringement of copyright subsisting in a person other than the State.

This is the only absolute exemption without invoking disclosure in public interest. In *UPSC v. CIC and Others*, the High Court of Delhi observed that under Section 9, the CPIO is empowered to reject a request for information where such a request for providing access to information would involve an infringement of copyright subsisting in a person. The power of the CPIO does not extend to rejecting such a request if the infringement of copyright involved belongs to the state.

# 'Public Interest Override' under Section 8(2)

Section 8(2): *Notwithstanding anything in the Official Secrets Act, 1923 nor any of the exemptions permissible in accordance with sub-section (1), a public authority may allow access to information, if public interest in disclosure outweighs the harm to the protected interests.*

All the ten exemptions under Section 8(1) are subject to the public interest test. This requires a decision-maker to weigh the public interest in maintaining exemptions and the public interest in disclosing the information. The RTI Act 2005 does not define 'public interest' and so is the case with other Freedom of Information Acts in the world. This has been done intentionally, so that determination can be made with regard to the specifics of each request. Decision-makers should give significant consideration to the public interest test when applying exemptions and identify in every case the specific public interest override in releasing particular information. The questions involved in identifying the 'public interest' are complex. Commercial interest's exemption is the hardest type of exemption to override in the public interest. When the release of third party personal information is subjected to a public interest test, it requires decision-makers to balance an individual's right to privacy with the public interest in release of the information.

In *Shiv Shambu and Others, Sanjeev Kumar and Others v. UPSC,* the full bench of the CIC considered a case of denial of information by UPSC regarding cut-off marks in the Civil Services Examination 2006. CIC ordered the disclosure. UPSC filed an appeal in High Court of Delhi. Justice Badar Durrez Ahmad in *UPSC v. Central Information Commission & Others*, held that Section 8(2) indicates access to information if the public interest in disclosure outweighs the harm to the protected interests. The disclosure of information as directed by the CIC, does not, in any way, harm the protected interests of the UPSC or any third party. In any event, the public interest in disclosure is overwhelming.

## Seven out of Ten Exemptions Listed in Section 8(1) not Valid after 20 Years under Section 8(3)

Section 8(3): *Subject to the provisions of clauses (a), (c) and (i) of sub-section (1), any information relating to any occurrence, event or matter which has taken place, occurred or happened twenty years before the date on which any request is made under section 6 shall be provided to any person making a request under that section:*

> Provided that where any question arises as to the date from which the said period of twenty years has to be computed, the decision of the Central Government shall be final, subject to the usual appeals provided for in this Act.

In *Sayantan Dasgupta v. Ministry of Home Affairs*, the full bench of the Commission held that a plain reading of Section 8(3) makes it clear that a public authority is obliged to provide information which is more than 20 years old. This is an obligation subject only to the provisions of clauses (a), (c), and (i) of Section 8(1) of the RTI Act. In all other cases, even though they may fall within the ambit of Section 8(1), the disclosure by the public authority is mandatory.

## Partial Disclosure

Records of information, such as documents, may contain both exempt and non-exempt information.

Section 10 of the RTI Act provides that where a request for access to information is rejected on the ground that it is in relation to information which is exempt from disclosure, access may be provided to that part of the record 'which does not contain any information which is exempt from disclosure under the Act' and 'which can reasonably be severed from any part that contains exempt information'.

Where access is granted to a part of the record, the Public Information Officer shall give a notice to the applicant under Section 10(2), informing that only a part of the record requested is being provided and the applicant has the right to review the decision with the Appellate Officer.

In this context, a full bench decision of CIC in *Nusli Wadia v. Ministry of External Affairs* is relevant.

# Non-applicability of the RTI Act 2005 to Organizations Listed in the Second Schedule

Section 24(1) of the RTI Act reads as: *Nothing contained in this Act shall apply to the intelligence and security organisations specified in the Second Schedule, being organisations established by the Central Government or any information furnished by such organisations to that Government:*

> Provided that the information pertaining to the allegations of corruption and human rights violations shall not be excluded under this sub-section.
>
> Provided further that in the case of information sought for is in respect of allegations of violation of human rights, the information shall only be provided after the approval of the Central Information Commission, and notwithstanding anything contained in Section 7, such information shall be provided within forty-five days from the date of the receipt of request.

At present, there are 25 organizations established by the central government which are listed in Schedule II of the Act. The details of the same are:

1. Intelligence Bureau.
2. Research and Analysis Wing of the Cabinet Secretariat.
3. Directorate of Revenue Intelligence.
4. Central Economic Intelligence Bureau.
5. Directorate of Enforcement.

6. Narcotics Control Bureau.

7. Aviation Research Centre.

8. Special Frontier Force.

9. Border Security Force.

10. Central Reserve Police Force.

11. Indo-Tibetan Border Police.

12. Central Industrial Security Force.

13. National Security Guards.

14. Assam Rifles.

15. Sashtra Seema Bal.

16. Directorate General of Income Tax (Investigation).

17. National Technical Research Organisation.

18. Financial Intelligence Unit, India.

19. Special Protection Group.

20. Defence Research & Development Organisation.

21. Border Road Development Board.

22. National Security Council Secretariat.

23. Central Bureau of Investigation (CBI).

24. National Intelligence Agency (NIA).

25. National Intelligence Grid (NATGRID).

It may be noted that to begin with, there were 18 organizations listed in Schedule II.

Information pertaining to identity of foreign account holders of Indian citizens from Directorate of Enforcement, an organization listed in Schedule II has been subjected to CIC and Court decisions. First, the CIC, in *V.R. Chandran v. Directorate of Enforcement*, looked into it. The full bench of the CIC held:

> ... We would like the matter to be taken beyond technicalities and to address the larger issue related to transparency in this vital field, about which the citizens of our country are keen for answers.... All matters now investigated by the Enforcement Directorate in the matter of stashing away of money in foreign banks, come within definition of allegations of corruption in Section 24.

It ruled that parties name may not be given, but information regarding awareness of that the government about existence of such secret accounts in Swiss banks amounting to $1,456 billion, and action taken in the matter, to be given. However, a writ petition was filed in High Court of Delhi, and the CIC decision was put on hold.

Also, the Supreme Court of India passed an order in *Ram Jethmalani and Others v. Union of India*:

79(i)   The Union of India shall forthwith disclose to the Petitioners all those documents and information which they have secured from Germany, in connection with the matters discussed above, subject to the conditions specified in (ii) below;

(ii)   That the Union of India is exempted from revealing the names of those individuals who have accounts in banks of Liechtenstein, and revealed to it by Germany, with respect of who investigations/enquiries are still in progress and no information or evidence of wrongdoing is yet available;

(iii)   That the names of those individuals with bank accounts in Liechtenstein, as revealed by Germany, with respect of whom investigations have been concluded, either partially or wholly, and show cause notices issued and proceedings initiated may be disclosed.

In another case, *Subhash Chandra Agrawal v. Directorate of Enforcement*, the appellant had filed an RTI application seeking information on secret accounts of

Indian citizens in Swiss banks and other several matters connected with it. The information was denied on the grounds that the Directorate of Enforcement is exempted under Section 24 of the RTI Act. The Commission held that given the totality of the circumstances and the peculiar facts of the present case, such information clearly pertains to 'allegation of corruption' under the First Proviso to Section 24 of the RTI Act. The Enforcement Directorate can surely provide an estimate of total volume of such money involved in their investigations.

# 7

# Recommendations to Improve Implementation of Right to Information

Right to Information (RTI) laws grant citizens the legal right to access information held by public authorities, bringing transparency in an otherwise opaque system. Globally, more than 80 countries have enacted such laws. India enacted such a law in 2005, following a nationwide campaign led by grass-roots and civil society organizations. India's RTI Act 2005 is internationally recognized as a strong and effective law. For about the last seven years, the law has been used extensively by ordinary citizens, social activists, and civil society organizations to redress individual grievances, access entitlements such as ration cards, investigate government policies and decisions, and expose corruption.

After the onset of economic reforms in 1991 the operation of the liberalized economy has vastly expanded the arena of discretion of the executive—both political and bureaucratic—causing an exponential rise in number and scale of malpractices. This was evident in the allocation of 2G spectrum, Commonwealth Games, and the mining scams in Karnataka and Orissa. Many of the controversies have been unearthed using the RTI Act. This calls for the elimination of discretion of civil servants and ministers, and laying down transparent procedures for decision-making. In this, effective laws and institutions are extremely significant in preventing corrupt practices and punishing those who commit them. It is here that the RTI law and the institution of Lok Pal can play a significant role. It is interesting to note that the BJP, the main opposition party, has an RTI Cell that operates at both the central and state levels.

What can be included in the definition of 'Information' and whether 'File Notings' are included in it, and what all organizations/offices are included in 'public authority' under the Act, has been subject of many controversies.

## Disclosure of File Notings

The draft RTI Bill received from the National Advisory Council (NAC) had mentioned file notings to be disclosed. But the Group of Ministers, as well as the Department-related Parliamentary Standing Committee, excluded file notings liable for disclosure. As such, right from the beginning, the Government held this belief that the 'note' portion of files should not be disclosed. Although the President had assented to the RTI Act, he cautioned the Government that the definition of words 'information' in Section 2(f); 'record' in Section 2(i); and ' right to information' in Section 2(j) are such that file notings can be asked. This he said:

> ... is not a fair approach and will harm the process of decision making as officials would be more cautious in or even refrain from rendering objective, frank and written advice on file. Sharing of information on decisions taken and sharing of information on

how the decision is actually arrived at have entirely different dimensions and ought to have been handled differently.

However, in view of sustained pressure of civil society organizations and decisions of Information Commissions, the Government had to issue administrative orders in 2009 for the disclosure of file notings. But as late as October 2011, the Prime Minister, while delivering the inaugural address at the Annual Convention of Central Information Commission, again raised the concern that RTI could end up discouraging honest, well-meaning public servants from fully expressing their views, as a point of view brought under public scrutiny and discussion in an isolated manner may sometimes present a distorted or incomplete picture of what really happened in the processes of making the final decisions. He cautioned that the RTI should not adversely affect the deliberative processes in the government.

It may be noted that Freedom of Information Act 2002, passed during the tenure of NDA Government did not allow disclosure of file notings. Also, many legislations enacted in the developed countries like the USA, UK, Australia, France, Netherlands, and Canada have exempted the 'deliberative process' from disclosure.

But all said and done, disclosure of file notings would help ensure that officers are not pressurized into recording notes that are not in public interest. This strengthens the hands of honest and conscientious officers and exposes the dishonest and self-serving ones. Disclosure of file notings will also improve the quality of decision-making, for it would ensure that decisions are based on reasonable grounds and not arbitrary or self-serving. It would deter bosses from overruling their subordinates and making unscrupulous decisions.

## Whether Chief Justice of India and Governor of a State are a 'Public Authority'

In 2007, an RTI application was filed with the Supreme Court asking, among other things, whether Supreme Court judges and High Court judges are submitting information about their assets to their respective chief justices. This information was denied on the ground that Supreme Court and the Chief Justice of India

(CJI) are outside the purview of the RTI Act. The full bench of the Central Information Commission held in *Subhash Chandra Agrawal v. Supreme Court of India* that both come within the Act. The Supreme Court filed an appeal in High Court of Delhi, where a single judge upheld the CIC decision. However, the Supreme Court filed an appeal against the single bench decision. The larger bench of the High Court, in its decision in January 2010, confirmed that the CJI is a public authority and the RTI Act covers the office of CJI. The Supreme Court took somewhat unusual and perhaps unprecedented step of filing an appeal against the order of the Delhi High Court in front of itself. It is interesting to note that even when the appeal against the single judge order was pending before the larger bench of High Court of Delhi, the CJI wrote to the Prime Minister for exclusion of CJI from RTI.

In another case, the Governor of Goa has moved the Supreme Court of India against a November 2011 order of the Bombay High Court claiming that he is not a public authority. The main argument is that Governor is Head of the State and is not subordinate to any entity. However, it is felt that the Governor's office should fall within the ambit of 'public authority'.

## Implementation Status of RTI Act

Two studies to assess implementation of the RTI Act were done in 2008–9. One was done by PricewaterhouseCoopers (PwC), under the aegis of the Government of India, and the other by people's organizations (RaaG and NCPRI). Both studies brought out the need to significantly improve proactive disclosure and record management. The studies concluded that awareness about the RTI Act was still very low, especially among rural populations and among women. Surveys done in rural areas as a part of People's Assessment estimated that in first two-and-a-half years of the RTI regime (October 2005 to March 2008) there were an estimated two million RTI applications of which about 400, 000 applications were filed from the rural areas, belying the assumption that only educated urban people use the RTI Act. Both studies concluded that the law was primarily used by men and only 5 per cent of the rural and 10 per cent of the urban applicants were women.

Harassment of applicants, particularly in rural areas, by public information officers, was highlighted by both the studies. In many cases the applicants had to visit the public authority office more than once to get their request accepted. There have been cases of applicants being discouraged from filing RTI applications, and even threatened or physically attacked.

# Recommendations to Implement Section 4

*a. Digitization of records by using mobile vans in rural areas.* Section 4(1)(a) of the RTI Act obligates every public authority to properly manage and speedily computerize its records. Replacing paper records by digital versions would make them less amenable for manipulation or loss. But this requires a strong push from the government. To create such facilities in a time-bound manner at the village level, mobile vans fitted with requisite facilities can be used.

*b. Implementation of Public Records Act.* Implementation of the Public Records Act 1993 has been appallingly ignored. This Act mandates management, administration, and preservation of public records of the Central Government and Union Territories. As such, large chunks of public information remain inaccessible to public. Also, there is no proper mechanism of declassification of government documents. Govern-ments around the world have mechanisms to declassify documents without imperilling their national inter-est. The Central Information Commission in *Sandeep Unnithan v. Integrated HQs, Ministry of Defence (Navy)*, had recommended

> ... Armed Forces of free democratic nations should have a proper disclosure of vital information policy in respect of events connected with engagements of our armed forces with the forces of other countries in theatres of war ... Indian Armed Forces should build up their storehouse of information under Section 4(1) of the RTI Act 2005 for disclosure at the appropriate time for the benefit of students of India's defence and to enhance the people's trust in the armed forces undoubted capacity to ensure national security.

*c. Periodic Updating of mandated proactive disclosure.* Compliance with Section 4(1)(b) which deals with proactive disclosure by public authorities should not be one time activity. It is important to make a particular official in a public authority responsible for its periodic updating.

*d. Enlargement of scope of proactive disclosure.* The President of India, while addressing the joint session of Parliament in October 2009, outlining the vision of the newly elected government, promised, 'a public data policy to place all information covering non-strategic areas in the public domain... (which) would help citizens to challenge the data and engage directly in governance reform.' This is much more than the 16 items which require proactive disclosure under Section 4(1)(b).

However, there are conflicting signals in this regard. A recent decision of the Supreme Court of India in *Central Board of India and Anr. v. Aditya Bandopadhyay and Others* (Civil Appeal No. 6454 of 2011) is relevant in this regard. It states:

> The right to information is a cherished right. Information and right to information are intended to be formidable tools in the hands of responsible citizens to fight corruption and to bring in transparency and accountability. The provisions of RTI Act should be enforced strictly and all efforts should be made to bring to light the necessary information under clause (b) of Section 4(1) of the Act which relates to securing transparency and accountability in the working

of public authorities and in discouraging corruption. But in regard to other information, (that is information other than those enumerated in section 4(1)(b) and (c) of the Act), equal importance and emphasis are given to other public interests (like confidentiality of sensitive information, fidelity and fiduciary relationships, efficient operation of governments, etc). Indiscriminate and impractical demands or directions under RTI Act for disclosure of all and sundry information (unrelated to transparency and accountability in the functioning of public authorities and eradication of corruption) would be counter-productive as it will adversely affect the efficiency of the administration and result in the executive getting bogged down with the non-productive work of collecting and furnishing information. The Act should not be allowed to be misused or abused, to become a tool to obstruct the national development and integration, or to destroy the peace, tranquillity and harmony among its citizens. Nor should it be converted into a tool to oppression or intimidation of honest officials striving to do their duty. The nation does not want a scenario where 75% of the staff of public authorities spends 75% of their time in collecting and furnishing information to applicants instead of discharging their regular duties. The threat of penalties under the RTI Act and the pressure of the authorities under the RTI Act should not lead to employees of a public authorities prioritising ' information furnishing', at the cost of their normal and regular duties. (para 37)

However, to start with, all RTI queries and answers given (except where information relates to private matters) may be put in the public domain.

e. Bringing *Systemic Changes.* Heads of Public Authorities should periodically review the underlying cause for RTI applications, which may be due to say, delay in response, or discrimination in application of rules, or non-disclosure of information. Based on this review, systemic changes can be initiated by Public Authorities.

## Public Consultation and Debate on All Major Policy Issues

Section 4(1)(c) mandates every public authority to publish all relevant facts while formulating policies. However, the government should supplement this with public consultation and debate on all major policy issues. Had this been done, many controversial decisions could have been averted. Lately, the government has started this process in many cases.

## Raising Awareness about the RTI Act

Information regarding the Act and its relevance to the people should be imparted in along with information about other basic rights, highlighting how the RTI Act can be used to ensure access to these other rights. This would not only place the RTI Act in its larger social context but also raise awareness about other rights. Different methods can be used for spreading this message, such as, folk theatre, song and dance, radio, television, and the print media.

## Training of All Public Authority Officials

As all public authority officials are connected with RTI Act, one day training should be imparted. Also, every quarter, Ministry of Law or Ministry of Personnel, should bring to the notice of all public authorities important interpretations of law decided by Information Commissioners and Courts.

## Uniformity of Rules

Section 27 and Section 28 authorize appropriate Government [defined in Section 2(a) of the Act] and competent authority [defined in Section 2(e) of the Act] to make rules to carry out the provisions of the Act. This can result in umpteen set of rules. There should be uniformity of rules on most of issues, like fee for basic application, for acquiring documents and so on, and rules for filing appeals.

## Protection of RTI Applicants and Whistleblowers

Applicants, especially from weaker section of society are often intimidated, threatened, and even physically attacked when they try to file RTI applications. Media and Information Commissions should make note of this and take action. The Government can declare all post offices in the country as Assistant Public Information Officers, so that applicants need not approach any public authority to file an application, or institute a call centre like 'Jaankari', where a request can be filed.

Many RTI activists have been murdered in different parts of the country. Most of those killed were investigating irregularities in sectors such as mining, land, and local elections where corruption is rampant. Civil society organizations are now demanding that the government take concrete measures to protect the lives of such individuals. It is likely that a Whistle Blowers Act will be passed by the Parliament shortly.

# Epilogue

The Supreme Court of India in *Namit Sharma v. Union of India* passed a judgment on 13 September 2012 which upset the implementation machinery of the Right to Information (RTI) Act. In this case, the public interest litigation challenged the constitutionality of Sections 12 and 15 of the RTI Act 2005, dealing with appointment of information commissioners.

The court held that the information commission is a 'judicial tribunal' having the 'trappings of a Court'. It further held that the information commissions shall, henceforth, work in benches of two each, one of them being a 'judicial member', while the other an 'expert member'. The competent authorities were asked to prefer a person who is, or has been, a judge of a high court for appointment as information commissioners. It also directed that the Central Information Commissioner (CIC) at the centre or state level shall only be a person who is, or has been, Chief Justice of a High Court or a judge of the Supreme Court of India.

There are number of controversial issues in this judgment. First, to treat information commissions as judicial tribunals with 'the trappings of a court'. A plain reading of the preamble of the RTI Act 2005 and the 'Statement of Objects and Reasons' of the Freedom of Information (FOI) Act 2002 (the predecessor of the RTI Act 2005) makes it clear that the essential purpose of these two legislations is to make information available to citizens as convenient as possible. Second, the court has completely rewritten the provisions regarding qualifications for appointments to the post of information commissioners. In this, it has gone beyond what has been prescribed by the Act. Third, it laid down the procedure for deciding the second appeal by having two-person benches with one judicial member.

A huge fallout of this judgment will be cessation of the activities of the commissions until members with judicial backgrounds are appointed. Till the time, the judicial experts are appointed, the number of second appeals pending with the information commissions would rise exponentially. Further, there are practical problems of constituting such benches due to paucity of information commissioners and their varying retirement ages.

In our scheme of things, law-making is a prerogative of the legislature and the judiciary interprets the same. In case the law violates the basic structure of the constitution, the same can be struck down. By ruling on the methodology of working of the commission, that is, a two-member bench and its manning, there appears to be a case of judicial activism.

In this context it is stated that the Commonwealth Human Rights Commission (CHRI) has conducted a rapid survey on the background of information commissioners from 35 national/provincial jurisdictions around the globe and their finding was that several information commissioners would have law degree but few had practised as lawyers for 20 years and none had any experience as a judge in a court of law prior to appointment as an information commissioner.

The union government has filed a review petition in the Supreme Court. It is hoped that the Union of

India will argue the case better in the review that it did in the original petition and the court will address the issues emerging out of the earlier judgment as pendency of cases remain a big problem.

# Cases

## Introduction

State of Uttar Pradesh v. Raj Narain and Others, AIR 1975 SC 865.

S.P. Gupta v. Union of India, AIR 1982 SC 149.

## Towards Right to Information in India

Bennet Coleman and Co. v. Union of India, AIR 1973 SC 106.

Association for Democratic Reforms v. Union of India, AIR 2001 Del 126.

Union of India v. Association for Democratic Reforms, (2002) 5 SCC 294.

PUCL v. Union of India, (2003) 4 SCC 399.

S.P. Gupta v. Union of India AIR 1982 SC 149.

# Right of Information Seekers

Sreekumar S. Menon, General Secretary, Kerala Peoples' Forum v. Indian Audit and Accounts Department, Kerala, Appeal No. CIC/AT/A/2006/00662.

The Secretary, the Cuttack Tax Bar Association, Cuttack v. The Commissioner of Income Tax, Cuttack, Orissa, Appeal No. CIC/AT/A/2007/00410.

Poorna Prajna Public School v. CIC and Others, WP (Civil) No. 7265 of 2007, (Manu/DE/2577/2009).

Aakash Aggarwal v. Debts Recovery Tribunal, New Delhi, Appeal No. CIC/AT/A/2006/00446.

B.P. Srivastava, Editor, Sub Ki Khabar, Delhi v. Executive Engineer, PWD, Appeal No. CIC/WB/A/2006/00290-291.

Sanjay Singh v. PWD, Appeal No. CIC/WB/A/2006/00144.

Central Board of Secondary Education and Anr v. Aditya Bandopadhyay, Supreme Court of India, Civil Appeal No. 6454 of 2011.

Dr. Celsa Pinto v. Goa State Information Commission, Writ Petition No. 419 of 2007.

Subhash Chandra Agrawal v. DoPT, 3rd Adjunct Appeal No. CIC/WB/A/2008/00956.

Dr. R.K. Garg v. Ministry of Home Affairs, Appeal No. CIC/AT/A/2006/00363.

# Duties of Information Suppliers

National Stock Exchange of India v. Central Information Commission and Others, W.P. (C) No. 4748 of 2007, High Court of Delhi.

Ajay Hasia and Others v. Khalid Mujib Sehravardi and Others, (1981) 1 SCC 722.

Ramana Dayaram Shetty v. The International Airport Authority of India & Others, (1979) 3 SCR 1014.

Pradeep Kumar Biswas v. Indian Institute of Chemical Biology, (2002) 5 SCC 111.

V.T. Gokhale v. UTI Asset Management Company Private Ltd., Appeal No. 2624/ICPB/2008.

Raj Kumari Agrawal and Others v. Jaipur Stock Exchange Ltd. and National Stock Exchange, CIC/AT/A/2006/00684 & CIC/AT/A/2007/00106.

Subhash Chandra Agrawal v. Supreme Court of India, Appeal No. CIC/WB/A/2008/00424.

Sarbajit Roy v. Delhi Electricity Regulatory Commission (DERC), No. CIC/WB/A/2006/00011.

Raj Mangal Prasad, B.M.Verma v. NCCF and NAFED, F. No. CIC/AT/C/2007/00320 & F.No. CIC/AT/C/2007/00324.

DAV College Trust and Management Society and Others v. Director of Public Institution and Others, Civil Writ Petition No. 2626 of 2008.

V. Malik v. Indian Olympics Association, Appeal No. 163/ICPB/2006, dated 28 November 2006.

Indian Olympics Association v. V. Malik and Others, WP(C) No. 876/2007, High Court of Delhi.

Right to Information Act 2005, CIC/AT/D/10/000111.

Parminder Kaur and fifty Others, Complaint No. CIC/WB/C/2008/00115/LS.

Chetan Kothari v. Cabinet Secretariat, Decision No. CIC/SM/A/2011/000278/SG/12906.

Subodh Jain v. Deputy Commissioner of Police, New Delhi and Institute of Company Secretaries of India, Complaint No. CIC/WB/C/2007/00943 along with Appeal No. CIC/MA/A/2008/01085.

Bombay Stock Exchange v. Security and Exchange Board of India, CIC/SM/A/2011/001687.

K.K. Mahajan v. Office of Cantonment Board, Dagshai, Himachal Pradesh, Appeal No. CIC/AT/A/2006/00014.

## Information Exempted from Disclosure

Kamal Anand v. Central Board of Direct Taxes, No. CIC/AT/A/2007/00617.

S.C. Sharma v. Ministry of Home Affairs, Appeal No. CIC/AT/A/2006/00056.

K.M. Talera v. Cantonment Board, Pune, Appeal No. CIC/AT/A/2006/00193.

Vishwanath Poddar v. Ministry of Company Affairs, Decision No. 308/IC(A)/2006 File No. CIC/MA/A/2006/00188.

Priya Pal Bhante v. Rajya Sabha Secretariat, Appeal No. CIC/WB/A/2006/00818.

Manohar Parrikar and Others v. Accountant General, Goa, Orissa, and Punjab, Appeal No. CIC/AT/A/2007/00274.

N. Anbarasan v. Indian Overseas Bank, Chennai, Decision No. 286/IC(A)/2006.

S.K. Maheshwari v. Telecommunications Consultants India Ltd., Appeal No. 77/ICPB/2006.

Anil Kumar v. ITI, Bangalore, Appeal No. 25/ICPB/2006.

Dev Dutt v. Union of India and Others, (2008) 8 SCC 725.

Central Board of Secondary Education and Anr. v. Aditya Bandopadhyay and Others, Supreme Court of India, Civil Appeal No. 6454 of 2011.

Manoj Kumar Pathak v. CBSE, Decision No. CIC/OK/A/2008/00832/SG/0677.

Rakesh Kumar Singh and Others v. Lok Sabha Secretariat and Others, Complaint No. CIC/WB/C/2006/00223; Appeal Nos. CIC/WB/A/2006/00469 & 00394, Appeal Nos. CIC/OK/A/2006/00266/00058/00066/00315.

Sharda P. Meshram v. DoPT, Appeal No. CIC/WB/A/2006/00959 & 1078.

Jyoti Legha v. UPSC, Appeal No. CIC/WB/A/2007/00185.

N.M. Chavda v. UPSC, Appeal No. CIC/WB/A/2007/00311.

B.L. Goel v. AIIMS, Appeal No. 845/ICPB/2007.

Mangla Ram Jat v. Banaras Hindu University, Decision No. CIC/OK/A/2008/00860/SG/0809.

Arun Jaitely v. CBI, Decision No.157/IC(A)/2006, F.No. CIC/MA/ A/2006/00230.

Kuldeep Kumar v. Commissioner of Police, New Delhi, Appeal No. CIC/AT/ A/2006/00071.

Bhagat Singh v. CIC, WP(C) 3114/2007.

Nathi Devi v. Radha Devi Gupta, 2005 (2) SCC 201.

B.R. Kapoor v. State of Tamil Nadu, 2001 (7) SCC 231.

V. Tulasamma v. Sesha Reddy, 1977 (3) SCC 99.

C. Seetharamaiah v. Commissionerate of Customs and Central Excise, Appeal No. CIC/AT/A/2008/01238.

Dugesh Kumari v. Income Tax Department, File No. CIC/LS/A/2010/000685.

Kharak Singh v. State of UP, AIR 1963 SC 1295.

R. Rajagopal v. State of TN, AIR 1995 SC 264.

H.C. Verma v. Indian Oil Corporation, Decision No. 999/IC(A)/2007.

Mr. 'X' v. Hospital, AIR 1999 SC 455.

Rakesh Kumar Singh and Others v. Lok Sabha Secretariat and Others, Complaint No. CIC/WB/C/2006/00223, Appeal Nos. CIC/WB/A/2006/00469 & 00394, Appeal Nos. CIC/OK/A/2006/00266/00058/00058/00066/00315, dated 23 April 2007.

Manohar Singh v. NTPC, Appeal No. 80/ICPB/2006.

Er. Ranjan Das v. Swami Vivekananda National Institute of Rehabilitation Training and Research, Cuttack, Appeal No. CIC/OK/A/2006/00441.

UPSC v. CIC and Others, High Court of Delhi, WP(C) No. 17583/2006.

Shiv Shambu and Others, Sanjeev Kumar and Others v. UPSC, Decision No. 354/IC(A)/2006.

UPSC v. Central Information Commission & Others, High Court of Delhi, WP(C) No. 17583/2006.

Sayantan Dasgupta v. Ministry of Home Affairs, Appeal No. CIC/AT/C/2006/00087.

Nusli Wadia v. Ministry of External Affairs, Appeal No. CIC/OK/A/2007/001392.

V.R. Chandran v. Directorate of Enforcement, Appeal No. CIC/OK/A/2007/001392.

Ram Jethmalini and Others v. Union of India, W.P.(C) 176 of 2009.

Subhash Chandra Agrawal v. Directorate of Enforcement, Appeal No. CIC/AT/A/2010/001215/SS.

## Recommendations to Improve Implementation of Right to Information

Subhash Chandra Agrawal v. Supreme Court of India, Appeal No. CIC/WB/A/2008/00424.

Unnithan v. Integrated HQs, Ministry of Defence (Navy), Appeal No. CIC/WB/A/2007/01192.

Central Board of Secondary Education and Anr. v. Aditya Bandopadhyay and Others, Supreme Court of India, Civil Appeal No. 6454 of 2011.

## Appointment of Information Commissioners and Working of Information Commissions

Namit Sharma v. Union of India, Supreme Court of India, Writ Petition (Civil) No. 210 of 2012.

# References

## Freedom of Information:
## A Global Perspective

Aid, M. (2006), *Declassification in Reverse: The US Intelligence Community's Secret Historical Document Reclassification Program*, National Security Archive, George Washington University. Available at http://www.gwu.edu/~nsarchiv/NSAEBB/NSAEBB179/index.htm.

Baniser, David (2006), 'Freedom of Information Around the World 2006: A Global Survey of Access to Government Information Laws', 20 September, *Privacy International*. Available at http://ssrn.com/abstract=1707336 or http://dx.doi.org/10.2139/ssrn.1707336.

Mendel, Toby (2008), *Freedom of Information: A Comparative Legal Survey*. Paris: UNESCO, pp. 141–54.

Wadham, John and Jonathan Griffiths (2005), *Blackstone's Guide to the Freedom of Information Act, 2000*. Oxford: Oxford University Press.

# Towards Right to Information in India

Department-related Parliamentary Standing Committee on Home Affairs (2000), *78th Report on Freedom of Information Bill, 2000.* Available at www.http://164.100.47.5/book2/reports/home_aff/78th report.html.

Department-related Parliamentary Standing Committee on Personnel, Public Grievances, Law and Justice (2004), *Third Report on The Right to Information Bill, 2004.* Available at www.humanrightsinitiative.org/.../ai/parliamentary _comittee_report.pdf.

Mander, Harsh and Abha Joshi (1999), *The Movement for Right to Information in India: People's Power for the Control of Corruption.* New Delhi: Commonwealth Human Rights Initiative.

Mentschel, Stefan (2005), *Right to Information: An Appropriate Tool Against Corruption?* New Delhi: Mosaic Books.

# Right to Information Act 2005

Centre for Media Studies (CMS) (2010), *India Corruption Study, 2010.* Available at http://www.cmsindia.org.

Commonwealth Human Rights Initiative (CHRI) (2009), 'Compliance with the Right to Information Act: A Survey'. Available at http://www.humanrightsinitiative.org/publications/rti/compliance_with_rti_act_survey.pdf.

Daruwala, Maja and Venkatesh Nayak (eds) (2008), *Our Rights Our Information: Empowering People to Demand Rights through Knowledge*. New Delhi: Commonwealth Human Rights Initiative.

Kulkarni, Ashwin (2008), 'Governance and the Right to Information in Maharashtra', *Economic and Political Weekly*, 30 August, 43: 15–17.

Peisakhin, Leonid V. and Paul Pinto (2010), 'Is Transparency an Effective Anti-Corruption Strategy? Evidence from a Field Experiment in India', 23 September, *Regulation & Governance*, 4(3): 261–80.

PricewaterhouseCoopers (PwC) (2009), 'Understanding the Key Issues and Constraints in Implementing the Right to Information Act'. Available at rti.gov.in/rticorner/study-bypwc/key_issues.pdf and http://rti.gov.in/rticorner/studybypwc/Executive%20Summary.pdf.

RTI Assessment and Analysis Group (RaaG) (2009), 'Report of the People's RTI Assessment 2008'. Available at http://rti-assessment.org.

Sharma, Kiran, K.C. Malhotra, and Ravai Gupta (eds) (2007), *Action Research Villages: A Right to Information Campaign*. New Delhi: Development Alternatives.

Society for Participatory Research in Asia (PRIA) (2006), 'Tracking the Progress of Right to Information in 12 States'. Available at cic.gov.in/StudyReports.htm.

# Right of Information Seekers

Singh, Shekhar (2011), 'The Genesis and Evolution of the RTI Regime in India', *Transparent Governance in South Asia*. New Delhi: Indian Institute of Public Administration, New Delhi.

# Duties of Information Suppliers

*The Times of India* (2011), 'CIC's RTI Order on Pvt Schools Stayed', 24 September.

# Information Exempted from Disclosure

Banisar, David and Sinion Davies (1999), 'Global Trends in Privacy Protection: An International Survey of Privacy, Data Protection, and Surveillance Laws and Developments', *The John Marshal Journal of Computer & Information Law*, 38(1). Available at: http://ssrn.com/abstract=2138799.

# Index